MULTICULTURAL CHILD MALTREATMENT RISK ASSESSMENT

*M*ulticultural Child Maltreatment Risk Assessment provides detailed descriptions of child maltreatment assessment and key strategies for culturally informed risk assessment in families.

The book presents a new model for evaluating families that includes cultural competence, a conceptualization of adequate parenting, and strategies for reflective decision making. Chapters address a range of factors including race, ethnicity, religion, gender, and sexuality. Ten case studies, each including discussion prompts, challenge the reader to apply forensic evaluation techniques for effective and ethical decision making in complex and ambiguous cases. Both experienced mental health providers and students will come away from the book with a deeper understanding of child maltreatment and its effects, models and modes of assessment, and factors that place families at greater risk.

Vassilia Binensztok, PhD, is an affiliate professor at The Family Institute at Northwestern University and a certified forensic mental health evaluator with extensive experience working in the child welfare system, the family court system, and counseling adult survivors of childhood trauma.

MULTICULTURAL CHILD MALTREATMENT RISK ASSESSMENT

EFFECTIVE EVALUATION FOR DIVERSE POPULATIONS

Vassilia Binensztok

Routledge
Taylor & Francis Group

NEW YORK AND LONDON

First published 2022
by Routledge
605 Third Avenue, New York, NY 10158

and by Routledge
2 Park Square, Milton Park, Abingdon, Oxon, OX14 4RN

Routledge is an imprint of the Taylor & Francis Group, an informa business

©2022 Vassilia Binensztok

Library of Congress Cataloging-in-Publication Data
A catalog record for this title has been requested

ISBN: 978-0-367-46403-5 (hbk)
ISBN: 978-0-367-46404-2 (pbk)
ISBN: 978-1-003-02856-7 (ebk)

Typeset in Minion
by Newgen Publishing UK

This book is dedicated to all the children who go overlooked.

CONTENTS

FIGURES

TABLES

PREFACE

The idea for this book was born when I was consulting on a case under the jurisdiction of a local child welfare agency. The mother on this case felt she was the victim of cultural discrimination when her children were removed and continued to remain in out-of-home care despite the completion of her case plan services, including parenting classes, individual therapy, and family therapy. The mother alleged the agency unfairly judged her character and actions because of ignorance of her ethnic, cultural, and religious background. Having started my career as a child protection caseworker many years ago, I hesitated to discount the agency's judgment, understanding the complex nature and high volume of cases processed each year. Many parents who are guilty of abusing or neglecting their children are vociferous about their dislike and distrust of agencies, and can vehemently proclaim their innocence. The skilled worker knows to withhold judgment until all information has been investigated.

Yet, I had never worked on a case as ambiguous as this one. Two separate parenting evaluations indicated minimal to moderate risk and this mother underwent additional psychological and neurological evaluations which indicated either no pathology or were inconclusive. None of the providers or attorneys working on this case, including myself, felt comfortable giving a definitive recommendation for reunification. This was largely due to the ambiguous circumstances of the case details. All the parties working on this case genuinely wanted the best for the children but toiled over the decision at hand. The obvious nurturing bond between this mother and her children was observed by all parties, yet, other odd characteristics stood in the way of anyone recommending reunification with full confidence.

The case dragged on and I spent a great deal of time pondering how to draw the line in this grey area. While we all observed the same characteristics that gave us pause, we struggled to reach consensus on the threshold for dysfunction. I found myself asking, 'How dysfunctional must a parent be to have their children permanently removed? How functional must they be in order to have their children confidently returned from stable out-of-home placements?' I pored over the evaluations, coming across a reference to minimal parenting standards, but when I pulled the article myself, I found the author stated that while minimal parenting standards must be used, they are poorly and inconsistently defined. I searched the state child protection laws, and found information about what constitutes abuse, neglect, and abandonment, but little information about determining risk. Larger searches revealed there was no consensus on what made a parent just too dangerous or just good enough.

As I considered this, something else nagged at me. I heard this mother lament several times that her children would have been reunified, or never even removed, had the family still been living in the culturally diverse US city they hailed from, quite different from the more suburban, more homogenous area in which we live. I had to ask myself, 'Would this case turn out differently if we were in that city?' Granted, cultural factors were not the only variables affecting the outcome of this case, yet I could not help but wonder if case workers, therapists, evaluators, and attorneys who were more accustomed to working with an ethnically, racially, culturally, and religiously diverse population, as one would find in this particular city, would perceive these case facts differently. It was a possibility one could not rule out. Of course, it is not the city that changes one's perceptions but, rather, the exposure to diverse people and practices.

Ambiguous situations abound in child protection work and are further complicated by cultural factors. Despite my expertise in both child welfare work and research, I had previously encountered cases that pointed more clearly in one direction than the other. I found that in these most ambiguous cases, providers were more likely to rely on cognitive shortcuts or reach a stalemate completely. My goal in writing this book was to compile the best research, along with my clinical expertise, to answer the questions providers face in child maltreatment cases complicated by ambiguity and cultural factors. I hope this book serves as a guide for fair evaluation of all families, particularly those who are ethnoculturally diverse.

CHAPTER ONE

Introduction to Multicultural Child Maltreatment Risk Assessment

Despite the progress made in child protection laws and child development education in the last few decades, child maltreatment remains an all too prevalent occurrence. Though rates of child maltreatment have been declining, there were 674,000 cases of maltreatment reported in the United States in 2017, with the youngest children representing the largest part of this demographic (US Department of Health and Human Services Child Welfare Information Gateway, n.d.). Children under three had a maltreatment prevalence rate of 15 per 1,000, outpacing every other age range. In 2018, 1,770 children died of abuse or neglect in the United States, with the majority of cases (70.6%) being children under three (US Department of Health and Human Services Office of the Administration of Children and Families Children's Bureau, 2018).

Child protection has a rather short history as a concept in the United States. During the industrial era, many children were employed in dangerous conditions. These children were deprived of the right to a childhood, to attend school, and to a safe and adequate environment. Though some child cruelty laws existed in the early 20th century, no organized systems of child protection existed. The Keating-Owen Child Labor Act (1916) became the first federal law to limit how many hours a child could be made to work and a later law, the Walsh-Healy Act (1936), banned the purchasing of goods produced by child laborers. Yet, decades spanned with no comprehensive child protection laws until the Child Abuse Prevention and Treatment Act of 1974, the first United States law of its kind. This law bore the initiation of the Child Protective Services model and required states to form guidelines for child abuse prevention and intervention (Hyun & Adams, 2016).

The enactment of child protection laws has made this a topic with which all mental health and human services providers are now familiar. These providers, along with medical providers and teachers, join the list of mandated reporters, or those professionals whose professional license and ethical oath require them to report any suspected child abuse or neglect to their state's child protection agency. Providers who fail to do so risk legal and licensing ramifications, as they knowingly allow children to remain in a potentially harmful situation. In 2016, roughly 4.1 million reports of child abuse were made to child protection agencies in the United States, representing 7.4 million children (US Department of Health and Human Services, 2018). Yet, while 65% of these referrals were made by professionals, only 5.9% came from mental health providers.

Counselors and other mental health professionals cite numerous barriers to reporting suspected child abuse and neglect. These can range from limited knowledge and training to fears of breaching confidentiality. Many counselors are unfamiliar with the laws related to child abuse reporting and studies have found those practitioners who lack knowledge are less likely to report abuse (Bryant, 2009). Counselors often lack training in risk assessment, abuse reporting processes and protocols, as well as an understanding of what their duties entail. Counselors can struggle with breaking confidentiality, though it is indicated in these cases, and report difficulty determining if and when to file a report, citing a lack of confidence (Kenny et al., 2018). School counselors were found to report only one case per year, on average, and often failed to report suspected cases of abuse and neglect (Kenny & McEachern, 2002).

Besides the hindrances from insufficient knowledge and lack of confidence, multicultural issues are another confounding variable in the assessment and reporting of child abuse. Because child abuse and neglect are primarily social problems, meaning they cannot be defined in medical terms, assessment of these issues remains largely subjective. Even when there are clear protocols for assessment and reporting in place, these are still based on a – typically Western – societal understanding of what constitutes abuse. Additionally, when applying protocols for child abuse assessment and reporting, practitioners are subject to allowing their personal morals and values into their reasoning process (Gillingham, 2006). Even researchers in this field are prone to having their personal values interfere with their work (McDermott, 1996). When conducting an assessment of child abuse and risk in multicultural settings, clinicians are prone to making more Type I and Type II errors, or false positives and false negatives, respectively. In some cases, false positives are made when clinicians impose their own values when assessing practices that are culturally sanctioned. On the other hand, clinicians risk false negatives when using culture to excuse behaviors that are harmful to children (Fontes, 2005).

This text will inform counselors and other mental health professionals of the protocols used in assessing child maltreatment and risk of future harm. Decision making strategies are explored to guide providers and increase confidence in assessment and reporting. Particular focus will be given to how helping professionals can apply these strategies to effectively evaluate harm and risk for harm.

PURPOSE OF RISK ASSESSMENT

Child maltreatment risk assessment can serve several purposes. Referrals for risk assessments and parenting evaluations are often made to help professionals determine if a family needs intervention, the forms of intervention a family needs, if children should be removed from their parents, if it is safe for children to be reunified with parents, if it is safe to allow unsupervised visitation between a parent and children, and other reasons. To complete an assessment providers must determine both if harm has occurred and if there is risk of future harm. Harm is defined as any detrimental act inflicted on a child. This can include psychological abuse, physical abuse, physical neglect, and sexual abuse. Risk assessment is defined as objective assessment for the risk of future harm to a child. Assessing current or past harm is critical in gaging risk of future harm. Assessment findings and recommendations can also help other providers, like therapists, effectively conceptualize cases and select appropriate treatment goals and interventions.

BENEFITS OF RISK ASSESSMENT

Determining if children are at risk is an important step in providing early intervention services. Countless research studies have confirmed the short-term and long-term effects of childhood maltreatment, including chronic mental and physical health detriments (Kenny et al., 2018). Risk assessment is critical for preventing future harm as well as selecting mental health treatments and implementing early interventions. Early intervention has been cited as crucial for recovery from childhood maltreatment (Cyr et al., 2013).

There are many limits to determining child safety and risk for future harm. These include the evaluator's subjectivity, lack of clear global definitions of maltreatment, and the possibility for false negatives and false positives (Pecora et al., 2013). False negatives occur when there is no determination of risk or harm, but risk or harm exists. False positives occur when there is a determination of risk or harm, but no risk or harm exists. Effective assessment and decision making models serve to avoid such pitfalls and lead to a greater likelihood of identifying and responding to risk and harm.

RISK ASSESSMENT GOALS

The goals of risk assessment include determining if harm has occurred, determining risk of future harm, identifying risk and protective factors, and identifying possible interventions. Information collected about past incidences of maltreatment or family violence can help providers assess the current level of risk as well as which interventions are indicated. Some families can display many risk and protective factors simultaneously. For these families, accurate risk assessment can determine which preventative interventions can help decrease risk. Risk assessment is also a thorough and structured process which helps reduce provider subjectivity and bias. Increasing objectivity

Risk Assessment Goals

- Identify **current** or **past** maltreatment.
- Identify **risk of future** maltreatment.

- Identify maltreatment **risk factors**.
- Identify maltreatment **protective factors**.

- Identify **treatment interventions**.
- Identify **preventative interventions**.

- **Reduce subjectivity** in decision-making.
- **Respect** cultural factors and context.

Figure 1.1 *Risk Assessment Goals*

also applies in respect to cultural factors. The goal of risk assessment is not only to evaluate family functioning, but also to do so within the context of a family's culture. Goals are presented in Figure 1.1.

CHALLENGES IN RISK ASSESSMENT

Numerous challenges arise in the assessment of harm and risk. Challenges can include the confluence of symptoms and incidents, difficulties in assessing risk of violence using the base rate fallacy, provider lack of knowledge or subjectivity, and cultural factors. All of these factors interfere with the ability to make clear and objective judgements about the occurrence of maltreatment and the potential for future harm.

SYMPTOMS VS INCIDENTS

Assessing past and current maltreatment is necessary for evaluating risk for future harm. When assessing maltreatment, however, providers are often tasked with assessing symptoms rather than incidents. Childhood maltreatment events, including physical abuse, sexual abuse, exposure to family violence, and psychological abuse, are considered incidents. Incidents are difficult to identify and evaluate for their veracity and level of harm. Therefore, providers must resort to evaluating the resulting symptoms of these incidents, rather than the incidents themselves (Binensztok & Vastardis, 2019). Symptoms must be evaluated according to the guidelines of the Diagnostic and Statistical Manual-5 (DSM-5). Child maltreatment, however, does not constitute any psychological disorder outlined in the DSM-5, and the symptoms associated with it do not typically meet criteria for any DSM-5 Disorder. The diagnosis for posttraumatic stress disorder (PTSD) was created based on the symptom presentation of Vietnam War veterans, so children may exhibit some PTSD-related symptoms like an increased startle response and nightmares, but rarely meet all criteria for this diagnosis (Olafson & Connelly, 2012).

While diagnoses for Developmental Trauma and Complex Trauma have been proposed for inclusion in the DSM, these syndromes have not yet been formally recognized, leaving children who have experienced maltreatment with no associated diagnosis, limiting the ability for providers to identify and evaluate these children. Developmental Trauma and Complex Trauma diagnoses take into account the unique manifestations of traumatic effects on the developing brain and effects of trauma that is chronic or continuous.

The traditional PTSD diagnosis limits its focus on Type I traumas. These traumas are defined as single events such as sexual assault or being the victim of a crime. Conversely, developmental and complex trauma refer to Type II traumas, which include ongoing traumas like chronic periods of neglect, and multiple trauma occurrences like multiple incidents of physical harm (Hudspeth, 2015; Terr, 1991). Developmental trauma also takes into account the effects of traumatic events on a developing brain, while the traditional PTSD diagnosis was created for adults, whose brains are matured.

Finally, another confounding factor lies in whether or not children show symptoms, or how long it takes for symptoms to manifest. Symptoms that result from child maltreatment are difficult to assess in and of themselves, as their patterns change over the developmental course. Symptoms might manifest in one area of functioning, but only begin to affect other areas of functioning as the child ages. Some symptoms can take years to manifest and can manifest in unexpected ways, creating a barrier to assessment of harm and future risk (Binensztok & Vastardis, 2019).

COMORBIDITY

As challenging as it is for providers to distinguish incidents from symptoms and determine if symptoms point to signs of maltreatment, comorbidity is another roadblock to assessment. The symptoms children do display can be falsely attributed to a range of diagnoses or events (Binensztok & Vastardis, 2019). Multiple forms of maltreatment often co-occur. Children can endure both physical abuse, psychological abuse, and neglect. Additionally, they might suffer abuse at the hands of multiple people, who are not all located within the home. They can be subject to other forms of abuse, like bullying by peers, and exhibit signs of other mental disorders. These factors can influence each other and worsen the effects of each form of maltreatment. Comorbidity makes assessing the nature of maltreatment, and the contributing qualities of the families in which it occurs, extremely challenging (Stockhammer et al., 2001).

Children can also present with related mental health problems triggered by maltreatment. These symptoms and diagnoses can mask the effects of underlying abuse and neglect (Gilbert et al., 2009). Children who have been victims of maltreatment can often also display symptoms of many different mental health disorders, including depression, anxiety, and behavioral problems. Comorbid presentations can lead to confusion about the true precipitant of these symptoms (Binensztok & Vastardis, 2019).

BASE RATE FALLACY

A base rate refers to the general probability of an event occurring. The base rate fallacy refers to people's tendencies to ignore base rate data in favor of case-specific data. People are prone to overestimating or underestimating the probability that an event has occurred when they focus on current case-specific details and ignore the base rate probabilities (Argote et al., 1990). Additionally, base rate information is often sparse or unavailable in matters of child maltreatment (Righthand et al., 2003). The lack of base rate data and the tendency to operate under the base rate fallacy are hindrances in the judgment of maltreatment incidents and risk for future harm.

PROVIDER KNOWLEDGE AND SUBJECTIVITY

Lack of knowledge and use of subjective judgment present as barriers to effective assessment. Researchers found that poor reliability in decision making is rampant in child maltreatment assessments. In a review of studies examining child welfare decision making, Ruscio (1998) found that 48% of child removals were unnecessary, while 45% of children necessitating removals were left in their homes. Primary reasons for these mistakes were lack of education, variability of knowledge, and limited provider experience. Even when structured decision making protocols were available, child welfare workers struggled to apply them because of these limitations (Levenson & Morin, 2006).

Children can also make false claims, recant accurate claims, or have their memories tainted by leading questions. The provider's degree of knowledge and experience in asking questions, finding information, and decision making is critical for effective assessment. Studies have also shown that the provider's personal characteristics can factor into decision making as well. Workers who are younger, less experienced, who are childless themselves, and who themselves had a history of corporal punishment or abuse were found to be more likely to judge incidents as abusive and perceive higher risk (Brunnberg & Pećnik,

2006). Still, inconsistencies remain in this research, as other studies found providers who were survivors of trauma were less likely to perceive children as being at risk (Regehr et al., 2010). Additionally, disparities in what constitutes abuse exist between states and jurisdictions. What is considered abuse in one agency or jurisdiction might not be considered such in another (Gillingham, 2006). As inconsistencies abound in the literature and research, so do they in the evaluation and decision making processes regarding child maltreatment and risk for future harm.

CULTURAL FACTORS

Culture is a broad term that refers to a group's shared values, beliefs, traditions, and histories. This differs from race and ethnicity, in that people of a specific race or ethnicity can still vary in terms of cultural beliefs and values. A further exploration of culture, race, and ethnicity can be found in Chapter 7. Cultural factors often act as barriers to effective assessment in relation to both the cultural identities of the providers and clients. Jent et al. (2011) found that white child welfare workers were more likely to classify physical injuries as physical abuse. Brunnberg and Pećnik (2006) found that Croatian social workers were more likely to assess incidents as requiring child protection intervention than Swedish social workers. In a comparative study, Korean social workers were found to be more likely to recommend children be removed from their homes than US Army social workers, while the US workers listed removal as their last option (Hyun & Adams, 2016).

Decision makers' perceptions are critical to making accurate judgments about child maltreatment and risk for harm. Racial and economic factors have both been found to affect how providers make decisions. Mandated reporters are more likely to suspect and report abuse in lower socioeconomic status (SES) families, Black families, and Native American families (Fontes, 2005). Some researchers contend these discrepancies in reporting also exist because of disparities in socioeconomic status. Neglect is more likely to occur in lower SES homes, and Black, Native American, and Latino children are more likely to live in homes lacking economic resources and are thus more prone to experience or be suspected of experiencing neglect (Charlow, 2001). Researchers have pointed to the fact that non-white children are more likely to enter the foster care system and that Black children are less likely to be returned to their homes than white or Latino children (Charlow, 2001). Conversely, white teachers were found to be less likely to report abuse when it occurred in Black children. Possible reasons for this include being confused about cultural disciplinary methods and becoming accustomed to witnessing effects of neglect in students in lower SES schools (Fontes, 2005).

ASSESSMENT PARADIGMS

Paradigms vary, as do the perspectives behind decision making. Some argue for the subjectivist position, which states that the role of relationships and intra and interpersonal perspectives are paramount to effective assessment and treatment. Those who argue for the opposing objectivist position state that subjectivist models are too intuitive and unstructured, and themselves rely on controlled assessments meant to yield high predictability (Stroud & Warren-Adamson, 2013).

CONSENSUS-BASED VS ACTUARIAL MODELS

Another debated topic regarding risk assessment frameworks is the use of consensus-based vs actuarial-based models. Consensus-based models require providers to use their clinical expertise to compare specific case facts to the characteristics which have been accumulated and agreed upon by the clinical community with the goal of making predictions. Actuarial-based models use instruments that are constructed from data drawn from large samples, from which researchers identify the characteristics most commonly associated with harm and risk. Actuarial instruments demonstrate greater reliability than consensus-based strategies, though the use of clinical expertise is not discounted (Stroud & Warren-Adamson, 2013). Intuitive decision making, as used in consensus-based models, relies on the expert practitioner recognizing patterns, while analytic decision making, as used in actuarial-based models, uses structured checklists and instruments. Both intuitive and analytic forms of decision making are crucial to accurate risk assessments (Pecora et al., 2013).

NEED FOR MULTICULTURAL ASSESSMENT

Existing models, whether consensus-based or actuarial-based, often fail to take culture and context into account. This has been the main criticism of the objectivist framework as well. Researchers have argued that objectivist measures provide a narrow view of families in that they reduce families to data points, rather than focusing on the presentation more holistically (Stroud & Warren-Adamson, 2013). Both Schlonsky and Wagner (2005) and Schwalbe (2008) argue the need for what is referred to as a contextual assessment. A contextual assessment evaluates child and family functioning using structured decision making while integrating contextual factors. Lack of contextual assessment strategies might be a factor in why Western countries see an overrepresentation of child maltreatment reports among ethnic and racial minorities (Cyr et al., 2013).

Culture has becoming increasingly important in assessment as US demographics have changed rapidly due to immigration. These changes bring with them the integration of varying cultural traditions and practices (Nadan et al., 2015). As the population evolves, so must the view of what constitutes childhood and appropriate discipline, and the understanding of child maltreatment criteria. Nadan et al. (2015) write, 'Disproportionate and disparate representation of cultural, ethnic, and racial groupings in child welfare, primarily in Western, industrialized nations, has stimulated concerns about how best to serve diverse populations in child welfare systems' (p. 41).

Culture influences several domains of child maltreatment and risk assessment, including consensus on what is considered abuse, bias in reporting, variability in abuse manifestation, and barriers to disclosure. Cultural norms greatly influence child-rearing practices and which behaviors are considered abusive. For example, though corporal punishment has largely fallen out of favor in the United States over the past few decades, it remains a mainstay in the disciplinary practices of some cultural and ethnic groups (Kolhatkar & Berkowitz, 2014). In the United States, Black parents can rely on physical punishment more frequently than white parents as this form of discipline is more accepted in Black communities (Lorber et al., 2011). Though much research has been done on the detrimental effects of physical punishment, the majority of this research was conducted with middle-class Anglo families (Lansford et al., 2004), making the results of these studies less generalizable to different racial and ethnic populations (Kesner & Stenhouse, 2018).

Some researchers posit that the link between child corporal discipline and negative cognitive and behavioral outcomes might be moderated by race, ethnicity, and other contextual factors (Taylor et al., 2011). Yet, other studies have confirmed the detrimental effects of corporal punishment, regardless of culture or parental intent. While some argue that cultural factors can mitigate the effects of behaviors that can be considered abusive or neglectful in Western culture, the converse can be true, and providers can be prone to normalizing abusive acts in the name of cultural context (Fontes, 2005). Culturally competent care respects cultural practices without promoting universal tolerance of all cultural practices (Kolhatkar & Berkowitz, 2014).

Culture also affects risk assessment in terms of which children and families are reported. Racial and ethnic disproportionality has been documented in the child welfare system. Several possible reasons for this exist. Some excess reporting may be due to discrimination and racial and ethnic bias that exists with individual providers as well as in larger agencies. Systems themselves can contribute to this disparity through inequitable allocation of resources and services to multicultural families. More children and families of color live in lower SES homes, increasing their risk for maltreatment. Furthermore, research on what constitutes child maltreatment, as well as maltreatment prevention and interventions, largely ignores cultural factors, leading to increased confusion for service providers (Nadan et al., 2015). These variations in perception of child maltreatment have been referred to as global variability (Kolhatkar & Berkowitz, 2014).

Additionally, culture affects how child maltreatment symptoms manifest. As previously discussed in this chapter, providers cannot rely on evaluating only instances and events of maltreatment, but must also focus on assessing the resulting symptoms. People of various cultures are known to express emotional symptoms in ways that are different from the common Western conceptualizations of mental illness (American Psychiatric Association, 2013). For example, while Anglo Westerners typically exhibit anxiety and depression through pronounced cognitive and mood states, people of other cultures can express these syndromes through somatic symptoms (Chang et al., 2016). Externalizing behaviors like anger or sexualized behavior can also be perceived differently in different cultures (Cohen et al., 2001). These presentations can further confound the assessment of mental health symptoms resulting from maltreatment in multicultural families.

Finally, cultural barriers to disclosure can impede information finding efforts in assessment. Cultural norms often affect if an individual or family will disclose maltreatment as well as if they will seek help and how they will respond to prevention and treatment interventions (Kolhatkar & Berkowitz, 2014). Relevant cultural norms can include collectivism, taboos, modesty, virginity, honor, shame, patriarchy, women's prescribed roles, and religion (Fontes & Plummer, 2010). In some cultures, individuals can face consequences for disclosing maltreatment such as loss of family support (Fontes & Plummer, 2010). Additionally, as many racial and ethnic minorities have experienced discrimination and disenfranchisement in institutions, they can be more skeptical of disclosing maltreatment to an authority figure. For others, they might find themselves stereotyped as model minorities. This typically occurs with people from Asian cultures in that they are often stereotyped as the ideal minority in the United States. Fear of disengaging with these stereotypes can prevent people who associate with them from disclosing maltreatment (Kanukollu & Mahalingam, 2011).

CASE STUDY

Monique is a 12-year-old Black female middle school student who meets with her school counselor because of a referral for failing a test. Monique's grades have been declining since the beginning of the school year and she often falls asleep in class. Teachers have also noticed that Monique often wears worn clothing and has ungroomed hair. When asked about her grades and falling asleep in class, Monique states she is 'just tired' because she shares a room with her sister who often keeps her awake at night talking on the phone and watching videos. The school counselor meets with Monique to discuss her grades and her behavior. Monique states she would like to get better grades but seems to not pay attention when the counselor gives her tips and instructions on how to improve her grades. The counselor writes a note about Monique's grades and behavior and instructs Monique to bring it home to her parents to sign and return it the next day. The following day, the counselor meets with Monique and inquires about the note. Monique says her mother did not have a chance to sign it because she did not return home the previous night and her father does not reside in the home. The counselor asks why the mother did not return home and Monique states that her mother was at work and has a few jobs. The school counselor begins to suspect that Monique and her siblings are being neglected.

CASE STUDY DISCUSSION PROMPTS

1. Describe the signs that lead the school counselor to suspect Monique is being neglected at home.
2. Explain how race and cultural norms could factor into the process of assessing if Monique is being neglected.
3. Explain your conclusion about if Monique is being neglected, what the next steps would be, and if you would report this family to the child protective services agency.

SUMMARY

This chapter explored the purpose and goals of risk assessment. Challenges to assessment were discussed, including the base rate fallacy, the pitfalls of false positives and false negatives, and cultural factors. Decision making paradigms were presented, along with a rationale for assessing families through a multicultural lens.

REFERENCES

American Psychiatric Association. (2013). *Diagnostic and statistical manual of mental disorders* (5th edn). APA.

Argote, L., Devadas, R., & Melone, N. (1990). The base-rate fallacy: Contrasting processes and outcomes of group and individual judgment. *Organizational Behavior and Human Decision Processes, 46*(2), 296–310. https://doi.org/10.1016/0749-5978(90)90034-7

Binensztok, V., & Vastardis, T. E. (2019). Child abuse assessment strategy and inventories. In L. Sperry (Ed.), *Couple and Family Assessment: Contemporary and Cutting-Edge Strategies* (3rd edn). Routledge.

Brunnberg, E., & Pećnik, N. (2006). Assessment processes in social work with children at risk in Sweden and Croatia. *International Journal of Social Welfare, 16*(3), 231–241. https://doi.org/10.1111/j.1468-2397.2006.00456.x

Bryant, J. (2009). School counselors and child abuse reporting: A national survey. *Professional School Counseling, 12*(5), 333–342. https://doi.org/10.5330/psc.n.2010-12.333

Chang, M. X., Jetten, J., & Haslam, C. (2016). Cultural identity and the expression of depression: A social identity perspective. *Journal of Community and Applied Social Psychology, 27*(1), 16–34. https://doi.org/10.1002/casp.2291

Charlow, A. (2001). Race, poverty, and neglect. *William Mitchell Law Review, 28*(2), 763–790.

Cohen, J. A., Deblinger, E., Mannarino, A. P., & de Arellano, M. A. (2001). The importance of culture in treating abused and neglected children: An empirical review. *Child Maltreatment, 6*(2), 148–157. https://doi.org/10.1177/1077559501006002007

Cyr, C., Michel, G., & Dumais, M. (2013). Child maltreatment as a global phenomenon: From trauma to prevention. *International Journal of Psychology*, *48*(2), 141–148. https://doi.org/10.1080/00207594.2012.705435

Fontes, L. A. (2005). *Child abuse and culture: Working with diverse families.* The Guilford Press.

Fontes, L. A., & Plummer, C. (2010). Cultural issues in disclosures of child sexual abuse. *Journal of Child Sexual Abuse*, *19*(5), 491–518. https://doi.org/10.1080/10538712.2010.512520

Gilbert, R., Kemp, A., Thoburn, J., Sidebotham, P., Radford, L., Glaser, D., & MacMillan, H. L. (2009). Recognizing and responding to child maltreatment. *The Lancet*, *373*, 167–180.

Gillingham, P. (2006). Risk assessment in child protection: Problem rather than solution? *Australian Social Work*, *59*(1), 86–98. https://doi.org/10.1080/03124070500449804

Hudspeth, E. (2015). Children with special needs and circumstances: Conceptualization through a complex trauma lens. *The Professional Counselor*, *5*(2), 195–199. https://doi.org/10.15241/efh.5.2.195

Hyun, J., & Adams, S. R. (2016). A comparative study of child abuse risk assessment in the United States and Korea. *Asian Social Work and Policy Review*, *10*(2), 210–224. https://doi.org/10.1111/aswp.12091

Jent, J. F., Eaton, C. K., Knickerbocker, L., Lambert, W. F., Merrick, M. T., & Dandes, S. K. (2011). Multidisciplinary child protection decision making about physical abuse: Determining substantiation thresholds and biases. *Children and Youth Services Review*, *33*(9), 1673–1682. https://doi.org/10.1016/j.childyouth.2011.04.029

Kanukollu, S. N., & Mahalingam, R. (2011). The idealized cultural identities model on help-seeking and child sexual abuse: A conceptual model for contextualizing perceptions and experiences of South Asian Americans. *Journal of Child Sexual Abuse*, *20*(2), 218–243. https://doi.org/10.1080/10538712.2011.556571

Kenny, M. C., & McEachern, A. G. (2002). Reporting suspected child abuse: A pilot comparison of middle and high school counselors and principals. *Journal of Child Sexual Abuse*, *11*(2), 59–75. https://doi.org/10.1300/j070v11n02_04

Kenny, M. C., Abreu, R. L., Helpingstine, C., Lopez, A., & Mathews, B. (2018). Counselors' mandated responsibility to report child maltreatment: A review of US laws. *Journal of Counseling & Development, 96*(4), 372–387. https://doi.org/10.1002/jcad.12220

Kesner, J., & Stenhouse, V. (2018). Investigating the potential effect of race and culture on preservice teachers' perceptions of corporal punishment and its subsequent effect on mandated reporting. *Australian Journal of Teacher Education, 43*(11), 71–83. https://doi.org/10.14221/ajte.2018v43n11.4

Kolhatkar, G., & Berkowitz, C. (2014). Cultural considerations and child maltreatment. *Pediatric Clinics of North America, 61*(5), 1007–1022. https://doi.org/10.1016/j.pcl.2014.06.005

Lansford, J. E., Deater-Deckard, K., Dodge, K. A., Bates, J. E., & Pettit, G. S. (2004). Ethnic differences in the link between physical discipline and later adolescent externalizing behaviors. *Journal of Child Psychology and Psychiatry, 45*(4), 801–812. https://doi.org/10.1111/j.1469-7610.2004.00273.x

Levenson, J. S., & Morin, J. W. (2006). Risk assessment in child sexual abuse cases. *Child Welfare, 85*(1), 59–82.

Lorber, M. F., O'Leary, S. G., & Smith Slep, A. M. (2011). An initial evaluation of the role of emotion and impulsivity in explaining racial/ethnic differences in the use of corporal punishment. *Developmental Psychology, 47*(6), 1744–1749. https://doi.org/10.1037/a0025344

McDermott, F. (1996). Social work research: Debating the boundaries. *Australian Social Work, 49*(1), 5–10. https://doi.org/10.1080/03124079608411156

Nadan, Y., Spilsbury, J. C., & Korbin, J. E. (2015). Culture and context in understanding child maltreatment: Contributions of intersectionality and neighborhood-based research. *Child Abuse & Neglect, 41*, 40–48. https://doi.org/10.1016/j.chiabu.2014.10.021

Olafson, E., & Connelly, L. (2012). Child abuse assessment strategy and inventories. In L. Sperry (Ed.), *Family assessment: Contemporary and cutting-edge strategies* (2nd edn). Routledge.

Pecora, P. J., Chahine, Z., & Graham, J. C. (2013). Safety and risk assessment frameworks: Overview and implications for child maltreatment fatalities. *Child Welfare, 92*(2), 143–160.

Regehr, C., LeBlanc, V., Shlonsky, A., & Bogo, M. (2010). The influence of clinicians' previous trauma exposure on their assessment of child abuse risk. *The Journal of Nervous and Mental Disease, 198*(9), 614–618. https://doi.org/10.1097/nmd.0b013e3181ef349e

Righthand, S., Kerr, B. B., & Drach, K. (2003). *Child maltreatment risk assessments: An evaluation guide.* Taylor & Francis.

Ruscio, J. (1998). Information integration in child welfare cases: An introduction to statistical decision making. *Child Maltreatment, 3*(2), 143–156. https://doi.org/10.1177/1077559598003002008

Schwalbe, C. S. (2008). Strengthening the integration of actuarial risk assessment with clinical judgment in an evidence-based practice framework. *Children and Youth Services Review, 30*(12), 1458–1464. https://doi.org/10.1016/j.childyouth.2007.11.021

Shlonsky, A., & Wagner, D. (2005). The next step: Integrating actuarial risk assessment and clinical judgment into an evidence-based practice framework in CPS case management. *Children and Youth Services Review, 27*(4), 409–427. https://doi.org/10.1016/j.childyouth.2004.11.007

Stockhammer, T. F., Salzinger, S., Feldman, R. S., & Mojica, E. (2001). Assessment of the effect of physical child abuse within an ecological framework: Measurement issues. *Journal of Community Psychology, 29*(3), 319–344.

Stroud, J., & Warren-Adamson, C. (2013). Multi-agency child protection: Can risk assessment frameworks be helpful? *Social Work and Social Sciences Review, 16*(3), 37–49. https://doi.org/10.1921/3703160304

Taylor, C. A., Hamvas, L., & Paris, R. (2011). Perceived instrumentality and normativeness of corporal punishment use among black mothers. *Family Relations, 60*(1), 60–72. https://doi.org/10.1111/j.1741-3729.2010.00633.x

Terr, L. C. (1991). Childhood traumas: An outline and overview. *American Journal of Psychiatry, 148*(1), 10–20. https://doi.org/10.1176/ajp.148.1.10

US Department of Health and Human Services Child Welfare Information Gateway. (n.d.). *Child Abuse and Neglect Statistics.* www.childwelfare.gov/topics/systemwide/statistics/can/

US Department of Health and Human Services Office of the Administration of Children and Families Children's Bureau. (2018). *Child Maltreatment.* www.acf.hhs.gov/cb/data-research/child-maltreatment

CHAPTER TWO

Defining Child Maltreatment

As definitions of what constitutes abuse vary between states and across cultures, providers must take varying, sometimes conflicting, information into account to make decisions. Providers must be aware of the definitions of maltreatment and how those differ in terms of culture. Some cultural child-rearing practices can be perceived as harmful or unusual though they are harmless, while other practices might be culturally sanctioned but universally deemed harmful. Many child rearing and disciplinary practices fall into a grey area in terms of harm. Parental intent is sometimes considered, particularly in terms of cultural views on discipline and parenting. Ultimately, maltreatment laws aim to standardize decision making processes by providing more universal definitions and protocols.

DIFFERING VIEWS ON CHILD MALTREATMENT

There are few universal guidelines on what constitutes maltreatment, and guidelines that do exist typically address more extreme and obvious forms of maltreatment. Many still argue for the use of corporal punishment as a form of discipline, bringing in the question of parental intent as a moderator. Because corporal punishment is viewed as acceptable by parents of different cultural origins, researchers wonder if the cultural normalcy of the act diminishes its ill effects. Federal and state laws attempt to define maltreatment more objectively, but statutes can still vary.

DISCIPLINE VS MALTREATMENT

Views on child discipline are largely dependent on cultural norms. Many parents of different cultures, including Anglo Westerners, view physical punishment as an effective form of discipline despite its well-known deleterious effects. Legally, in the United States, physical punishment is not viewed as abusive unless visible marks are left on a child, though researchers have come to a consensus on the deleterious effects of physical punishment.

PARENTAL INTENT

Providers often wonder whether or not to label a behavior as abusive when met with the factor of the parent or caregiver's intent. Many parents might claim that their behavior toward their children was not intended to harm. The claim is usually that the behavior was meant to discipline the child and that the parent was ignorant to the harm they could cause. While, for many, this can be true, intent does little to moderate the harm experienced by children. Though some practitioners argue that intent should be taken into account, it is clear that these behaviors are still harmful, whether or not they were done inadvertently (World Health Organization, 2002).

US CHILD MALTREATMENT LAWS

Child maltreatment is defined by both federal and state laws. Claims of maltreatment are investigated by state-run agencies and can be defined in both civil and criminal law statutes. The Federal Child Abuse Prevention and Treatment Act (2010) intended to provide more standard definitions and recommendations for preventing and responding to child maltreatment. Still, legislation is enacted at the state level and definitions of what constitutes abuse can vary between states. For example, not all states address issues like parental substance use disorders, and only 15 states include human trafficking under their definitions of physical abuse (Child Welfare Information Gateway, 2019).

FORMS OF MALTREATMENT

While there are a lack of universal laws and definitions regarding child maltreatment, there is still consensus about which acts are considered maltreatment. Categories of child maltreatment include physical abuse, sexual abuse, psychological abuse, neglect, abandonment, and provision of an unsafe living environment. Different acts can fall across several categories. For example, deliberate and cruel restraint of a child can fall into both the physical abuse and psychological abuse categories. The following descriptions of these acts represent definitions similar to those of state and federal laws, though categories and details can vary from one jurisdiction to the next. Table 2.1 outlines the various forms of abuse and neglect.

PHYSICAL ABUSE

Physical abuse is defined as any 'nonaccidental physical injury to the child' (Child Welfare Information Gateway, 2019, p. 1). Acts of physical abuse can include hitting with a hand, hitting with a stick, strap, or other object, kicking, choking, punching, stabbing, burning, biting, shaking, throwing, or any other physical act resulting in harm or impairment. These acts can result in visible harm, physical impairment, or create risk of harm when combined with other abusive acts (Righthand et al., 2003). Tying, binding, or physically restraining children crosses both the physical abuse and psychological abuse categories.

SEXUAL ABUSE

Sexual abuse definitions include three behaviors: intrusion, genital molestation, and other/unspecified acts of sexual abuse (Righthand et al., 2003). Intrusion refers to any oral, vaginal, or anal penetration. Penetration can be digital, penile, or unspecified, i.e. using objects. Genital molestation refers to genital contact, like fondling, without penetration. Other and unspecified acts refer to acts that do not involve genital contact, like fondling breasts or buttocks, or exposing one's genitals. These acts can also include voyeurism and intentionally showing pornography to children. Sexual exploitation falls under this category as well and includes coercing children into prostitution and creating child pornography (Child Welfare Information Gateway, 2019).

PSYCHOLOGICAL ABUSE

Psychological abuse, also known as emotional abuse, is any act that causes mental or emotional injury to a child. These acts include psychological injuries that cause emotional distress, changes in psychological capacity or emotional stability, and changes in behavioral, cognitive, or emotional responses (Child Welfare Information Gateway, 2019). Verbal abuse can include belittling, scapegoating, denigrating, threatening, and rejecting. Psychological abuse can also be attributed to related acts like attempted physical or sexual assaults, throwing something at a child without striking them, involving a child in illegal activity, and withholding sleep, food, shelter, or other necessities. As previously mentioned, physical acts such as binding or restraining a child can be considered acts psychological abuse, as well as confining a child to a closed or inappropriate area like a closet, basement, or cage.

The following acts have been defined by researchers as most commonly encompassing psychological abuse: (1) spurning, or using verbal and emotional assaults that include patterns of belittling, denigrating, non-physical degrading; (2) terrorizing, or threatening to physically hurt, kill, or abandon a child, threatening to hurt a child's loved ones or pets, exposing a child to danger and violence, including intimate-partner violence; (3) exploiting or corrupting a child by encouraging deviant or delinquent behaviors, parentifying or infantilizing a child, or engaging a child in illegal activity; (4) isolating or withholding emotional responses including ignoring a child's need and desire to interact, withholding love and affection, placing unreasonable restrictions on a child's social interactions, and interfering with healthy peer or adult relationships; (5) punishments that include binding a child or confining a child to a closed area, including prolonged confinement; (6) other abuses including attempted physical or sexual assaults, withholding food, shelter, sleep, and other necessities (Hart et al., 2002; Righthand et al., 2003; Sedlack & Broadhurst, 1996).

NEGLECT

Neglect refers to the failure to provide for a child's safety, physical, emotional, and educational needs. Parents can fail to provide food, shelter, clothing, or medical care. Medical neglect specifically refers to failure to seek appropriate and timely medical services, and failure to provide medical care recommended by professionals. Educational neglect refers to failures to respond to a child's developmental needs, to enroll or send a child to school, to make sure a child arrives at school on time, or to attend to other educational needs. Other forms of physical neglect include failure to provide nutrition, failing to meet a child's hygiene needs, and ignoring possible safety hazards. Physical neglect also refers to inappropriate supervision of a child, leaving a child in the care of an inappropriate or inadequate caregiver, and leaving a child unsupervised (Righthand et al., 2003).

Psychological neglect can include exposing a child to harmful conditions or illegal activities. Psychological neglect also encompasses failure to seek appropriate treatment and intervention for a child's substance use problems, mental health problems, and behavioral problems (Righthand et al., 2003). Additionally, psychological neglect refers to behaviors like failing to attend to developmental and emotional needs, failing to provide adequate attention and interaction, and failing to notice or inquire about a child's emotional and psychological needs.

ABANDONMENT

Abandonment refers to a parent expelling a child from the home with no provision for shelter or care, or leaving a child without returning. The parent might leave a child with others while the parent's identity or whereabouts remain unknown. The parent might fail to retrieve a child from school, or from an institution, such as a mental health or juvenile delinquency center, refusing to take custody of a child. Additionally, abandonment occurs when a child is left with caregivers who could cause harm or when a parent fails to keep contact with a child or provide essential support for an extended period of time (Child Welfare Information Gateway, 2019).

UNSAFE LIVING ENVIRONMENT

Unsafe living environments are typically classified under the categories of physical abuse, neglect, and abandonment in most US laws. These environments could include an unsanitary or unsafe home, exposure to substances and substance use, exposure to illegal activities, exposure to domestic violence, and failure to protect from physical or sexual abuse. Unsanitary or unsafe homes may be extremely unclean, leave chemicals, cleaning agents, or medications within reach of children, or have exposed wiring or other hazards. Some homes can be filled with clutter due to hoarding, leaving children with no room to sleep or play, or blocking emergency exits. Others might have uncontrolled infestations of roaches, rodents, or other pests.

Parent substance use can put children in unsafe scenarios as well. Parents under the influence can neglect or endanger a child by driving under the influence or creating a hazard in the home, i.e. a fire. Mothers with substance use problems can use substances while a fetus is in utero. Parents might leave dangerous substances within reach of children, manufacture drugs in the home, sell drugs from the home, or invite house guests that could be a danger to children (Child Welfare Information Gateway, 2019).

Parents can expose children to domestic violence through witnessing intimate partner violence, or any other violence in the home. Parents can be guilty of failure to protect when they knowingly leave children in the care of people who could be a danger to children. This can include knowingly allowing someone who sexually abused a child(ren) to stay in the home, or leaving children with people who are known to have physically or sexually abused a child in the past.

Table 2.1 Forms of Abuse and Neglect

Physical Abuse	Hitting with a hand Hitting with objects (stick, strap, etc.) Kicking Punching Choking Stabbing Burning Biting Shaking Throwing Binding/tying/restraining
Sexual Abuse	Intrusion: oral, anal, or vaginal penetration Genital molestation: genital contact without penetration Other/unspecified: fondling breasts or buttocks, exposing genitals, voyeurism, showing pornography Sexual exploitation: child prostitution, child pornography
Psychological Abuse	Verbal abuse: belittling, scapegoating, denigrating, threatening, rejecting, degrading Terrorizing: threatening to hurt or kill (child, loved ones, or pets), exposure to danger, exposure to violence Exploiting: encouraging deviant/delinquent behavior, parentifying, infantilizing, engaging child in illegal activity Isolating from social and emotional interactions Withholding love, affection, interaction, and emotional responses Binding/tying/restraining Confining to a closet, basement, etc. Attempted physical or sexual assault Withholding food, shelter, sleep, etc.
Neglect	Physical neglect: failing to provide food, shelter, clothing, hygiene needs, etc. Medical neglect: failing to provide medical services and care Educational neglect: failing to enroll in school, ignoring educational and developmental needs Ignoring safety hazards Inappropriate supervision or caregiver placement Failure to seek appropriate treatment for child's substance use, mental health, or behavioral problems Ignoring a child's emotional needs
Abandonment	Expelling a child from home with no provision for shelter or care Leaving a child without returning Refusing to take custody of a child from school or other placements Leaving a child with caregivers that can cause harm Failing to keep in touch with a child or provide support for an extended period

Table 2.1 Cont.

Unsafe Environment	Unsanitary home: unclean home, pest infestations, etc. Unsafe home: exposed wires, chemicals, cleaning agents, or medications within reach of children, excessive clutter, etc. Exposure to substance use (parents using substances, substance use in utero, making substances in home, selling substances in home, substances within reach of children) Exposure to illegal activities Exposure to domestic violence Exposure to people who could be dangerous to a child Failure to protect children

CULTURAL FACTORS IN MALTREATMENT

Providers must take culture into account when assessing for child maltreatment and risk. Culture can influence how parents view their behaviors toward their children. Views on physical abuse, psychological abuse, physical neglect, and emotional neglect vary between countries. Yet, views can also be largely similar across cultures. Researchers found agreement in mothers across nine countries that physical abuse is perceived as most harmful to child development and emotional neglect is seen as least harmful (Mesman et al., 2020). Variations in cultural practices, child rearing practices, and views on discipline methods should factor into conceptualizations of acts toward children and whether or not they should be considered abusive. At the same time, providers must be careful not to use culture as a broad excuse for acts that are truly harmful to children (Fontes, 2005; Kolhatkar & Berkowitz, 2014). This discrepancy is addressed in writings about cultural relativism vs universalism.

CULTURAL RELATIVISM VS UNIVERSALISM

To make more accurate decisions, providers must navigate ideas of cultural relativism and universalism. Cultural relativism weighs the value of cultural practices and beliefs when determining if an act is acceptable or harmful. In order to avoid stereotyping and imposing the dominant culture's values, cultural relativism seeks to view all behaviors in a cultural context, rather than espousing a singular truth (Fowers & Richardson, 1996). Relativism respects different cultures and evaluates behaviors as they make sense within the culture from which they originate. This also means one culture cannot deem the practices of another culture as inferior. Cultural relativism has grown popular in the social sciences, particularly as a response to a historical practice of globalization, or imposing the ethnocentric and imperialistic values and Western practices across other cultures.

Universalism, on the other hand, posits that universal truths and morals exist, and that people across cultures can be held to the same standards. Though the helping professions have largely moved away from universalist ideas and toward culturally relativist ideas, some argue that universalism still plays an important role in our understanding of clients (Kinnier et al., 2008). Some researchers argue that certain cultural practices must be open for criticism from other societies. For example, if a culture enslaves people or engages in genocide, cultural relativism can dictate that these acts should be deemed acceptable because they are condoned under the guise of culture (Rachels & Rachels, 2015).

Many women have fallen victim to cultural practices that are masks for traditional hierarchy and patriarchy, and relativistic views of these practices have impeded efforts for women's rights in areas like Sub-Saharan Africa (Msuya, 2019). Fontes (2005) states that blindly using culture to justify behaviors can lead to more false negatives in assessment and that cultural practices must still be evaluated for harm. Additionally, the goals of doing no harm and alleviating suffering are universal counseling goals (Kinnier et al., 2008). In order to be effective across contexts, counselors must become comfortable with and adept at evaluating situations both within cultural contexts and through a universal lens, with the ultimate goal of minimizing harm to others.

HARMFUL CULTURAL PRACTICES

Certain beliefs and practices can be deemed unacceptable, even if they fall under the realm of cultural tradition. Though they may be accepted in some cultures, these practices should be evaluated in terms of the physical and psychological harm they cause. Included in this list are female genital mutilation, son preference, honor killings, virginity testing, and child marriage. The estimation of harm caused by these events might serve as a guideline for evaluating other cultural practices.

FEMALE GENITAL MUTILATION

Female genital mutilation includes the cutting of female genitals for non-medical reasons (World Health Organization, 2020). This practice is most often carried out in Sub-Saharan Africa, as well as regions in the Middle East and Asia, and it is estimated that over 200 million girls worldwide have undergone this procedure (UNICEF, 2016). Female genital mutilation is performed on girls, and children assigned female at birth, between infancy and 15 years of age, typically with no anesthesia and in unsanitary conditions. It includes the cutting of the labia minora and removal of the clitoris, or clitoridectomy. This is done using a variety of sharpened tools that can include stones and shells. The labia majora is then sewn shut, known as infibulation, with a small hole remaining for the passage of urine and menstrual blood. This practice is done in order to ensure girls are 'clean' and ready for marriage. Female genital mutilation causes psychological and physical damage often resulting in infections, sepsis, and reduced or eliminated capacity for sexual pleasure long after the pain of the procedure subsides. Although female genital mutilation is illegal under federal law in the United States, there have still been cases of this practice observed in the US (Mather & Feldman-Jacobs, 2015).

SON PREFERENCE

Son preference refers to the preference of having male children over female children in some cultures. This preference is most often seen in Southern and Central Asian Countries, North Africa, and Eastern Europe. Girls born into cultures that espouse son preference are at risk of neglect, early mortality, and unequal allocation of resources, breastfeeding and food, medical care, prenatal care, and attention from parents (Barcellos et al., 2010; Basu & de Jong, 2010; Glover & Liebling, 2017; Jayachandran & Kuziemko, 2011; Oster, 2009). In extreme cases, son preference can lead to female feticide, infanticide, and sex-determined abortion (Chen et al., 2013).

HONOR KILLINGS

Honor killing is the practice of killing a person in order to protect family honor. In cultures of honor, the concept of family honor is highly valued and family members can commit an act that is thought to bring shame or disgrace on the family. The family is considered to have protected their family name and dignity by killing the accused family member. This practice is most often observed in the Middle East, though it has been documented in the United States as well (Amnesty International, n.d.). Though anyone can be subject to honor killing, women are the most common victims. Acts said to dishonor the family include sex before or outside of marriage, being the victim of sexual assault, not accurately practicing religion or cultural traditions, and dressing immodestly (Goodwin, 2003). Men are most often victim to honor killings when they engage in same-sex sexual relationships, or are merely suspected of being attracted to people of the same-sex (Amnesty International, n.d.).

VIRGINITY TESTING

Virginity testing is the practice of examining a person's vagina to determine if the hymen is intact, thus hoping to determine if she has engaged in penetrative sexual intercourse. This practice is common in cultures around the world including some African nations, the Middle East, and South Asia. Though originating in these areas, virginity testing has also been observed in the United States (Gharib, 2019). To begin with, virginity testing is not an accurate practice as some women are born without a hymen and hymens can rupture in different ways including playing sports, being injured, or using tampons. A woman who has had intercourse can still have an intact hymen as well (Behrens, 2014). Thus, virginity tests can result in both false positive and false negative results. Virginity testing is an intrusive procedure that violates privacy and bodily integrity (Commission on Gender Equality, 2005). It is often performed by male family members or in large public gatherings. Women who are deemed to be non-virgins are typically known throughout the community and can suffer a range of consequences including stigmatization, ostracization, and honor killings, as families consider themselves humiliated by these results. Women who are deemed virgins can also face dire consequences like being vulnerable to rape as a punishment for spurning a love interest, or in communities that believe intercourse with a virgin can cure HIV (South African Human Rights Commission, n.d.). Besides being degrading and dangerous to women and girls, this practice perpetuates sexism and patriarchy, deeming some girls to be more worthy than others, based on their virginity (Behrens, 2014).

CHILD MARRIAGE

Child marriage is the formal marriage that results in sexual union of children under the age of 18. This practice is most commonly observed in Sub-Saharan African and South Asian cultures. Child marriage disproportionately affects girls, who are often married to older males. An estimated 700 million women who are alive today were married before the age of 18 and as many as one in three of these were married before the age of 15 (UNICEF, 2014). It is estimated that 50% of women in Malawi, aged 20–24, were married before age eight, as different cultural rules and practices predispose girls to child marriage in this country (Mwambene & Mawodza, 2017). Girls who are married before the age of 18 face a slew of psychological, physical, and educational disadvantages. Child brides are often expected to bear children in haste, suffering increased pregnancy complications, childbirth complications, and premature birth. Pregnancy and childbirth are considered the second leading cause of death for adolescent girls worldwide (WHO, 2014). Child brides are also denied the right to an education and vocation, placing them in more vulnerable and disempowered positions.

ACCEPTED CULTURAL PRACTICES AND GREY AREAS

Some acts must be understood within a cultural context, as they are not inherently harmful. Evaluating these events and behaviors through an entirely Western cultural lens can prove discriminatory, particularly with social science's history of imposing Western ideals on non-Western cultures. Failing to take culture into account can lead to false positives in maltreatment and risk assessment and disturb a healthy family unit. These include alternative sleeping arrangements, child discipline methods, and other cultural practices. Still, there is debate on the safety of some of these practices, and decision-making often has to occur within grey areas.

SLEEPING ARRANGEMENTS

People from different cultures can have sleeping arrangements for children and other family members that are not harmful but foreign to Westerners. Families originating from South America, Africa, or Asia often arrange for children to sleep on the floor. This could be due to custom or economic factors like not being able to afford beds or a crib. While this is uncommon for Western families, it is a practice that does not cause inherent harm (Fontes, 2005). Additionally, it is common for children and families to share a bed. Again, this could be attributed to economic reasons but also because it is customary to not let children sleep alone. While Westerners might be unfamiliar with this practice, people from South and Central American, Southeast Asian, and East African cultures typically balk at the notion that children in the United States sleep in rooms alone (Rogoff, 2003). Though co-sleeping is common in many cultures, it is still a primary factor in Sudden Infant Death

Syndrome (SIDS) (UNICEF, 2019). Children sharing beds or bedrooms with parents can also hear the sound of their parents' lovemaking and sexual intercourse. While this might not be frowned upon in some families, children can still be uncomfortable and experience this as abusive (Fontes et al., 2001).

CHILD DISCIPLINE

Disciplinary methods can also vary across cultures. In some families, children are punished by being made to kneel on grains of uncooked rice on the floor. In Spanish, this practice is known as 'hincar' (Fontes, 2005). This practice is commonly seen in Latin American, Asian, and Eastern European cultures. Though it can be painful, it is not well understood if this practice is experienced as abusive. While providers are cautioned not to conclude this act is abusive as it is extremely common in many cultures, particularly Latin American cultures, providers should keep in mind that any corporal punishment can be perceived as abusive, have the same detrimental effects as abuse, and serve as a major risk factor for future maltreatment.

Views on corporal punishment vary as well. Corporal punishment is seen as acceptable and even beneficial in many cultures, despite its documented ill effects. As many as 67% of respondents to a survey of Caribbean nations stated they view corporal punishment as a practice that helps children grow into successful well-functioning adults (Landon et al., 2017). Yet, as previously mentioned, mothers surveyed in different nations still often rank physical punishment as harmful (Mesman et al., 2020). Despite its well-documented adverse effects, some researchers theorize that the negative effects of physical punishment might be moderated by race (Taylor et al., 2011). Referred to as the normativeness perspective, the concept states that if physical punishment is used within a culture where it is accepted, it will be better received by children and perceived as less harmful. Corporal punishment is more highly endorsed by Black families than white families in the United States and effects on child behavior have been debated. Yet, in a study by Gershoff & Grogan-Kaylor (2016), physical punishment was related to adverse effects at similar rates for both Black and white children and no beneficial effects were found in relation to physical punishment. Therefore, physical punishment should be evaluated within a cultural context but still under the premise that it is harmful to children.

CULTURAL PRACTICES

Many practices seen in other cultures may be foreign or confusing to Westerners, but it does not mean they are inherently harmful. Those practices that do cause harm can often be mitigated with education on child-rearing practices, rather than more invasive measures. These can include different kinds of boundaries and expectations, hygiene and appearance, medical practices, and spiritual practices.

Some cultures welcome extended family into the nuclear family unit, a practice that researchers have called the familial self (Falicov, 1998). Most often seen in Latin American and Asian cultures, the familial self involves sharing resources, such as shelter, clothing, and food, with extended relatives and friends. While Western providers might be alarmed at the number of people in the home, or the comings and goings of many family members, this can be a completely acceptable and non-harmful practice (Fontes, 2005). Additionally, it is not uncommon for Black mothers to receive support in the form of a market-family matrix, in which siblings, extended family, and community members provide childcare and emotional support (Dow, 2019).

Many cultures have varying practices of hygiene, hair cutting, and dress. Some cultures have restrictions on bathing after certain occasions like childbearing, illness, or death of a loved one. In others, women are forbidden to bathe while menstruating. After the death of a loved one conservative and Orthodox Jewish people might not cut their hair, shave, bathe, or look in the mirror (Orenstein, 2000). In a religious practice known as Upsherin, Orthodox Jewish boys do not receive their first haircut at age three (Chabad, n.d.). Cultures including Native American, Rastafarian, and other ethnic groups can place restrictions on hair cutting as well (Fontes, 2005). While some might find these people to appear unkempt and suspect neglect, these are acceptable, and sometimes sanctified, cultural practices.

People from some cultures can be skeptical of Western medicine and can highly prize traditional cultural forms of healing. Some practices like cupping – using suction cups to relieve muscle strain and increase blood flow – can leave marks and bruises though they are harmless and not abusive (Kolhatkar & Berkowitz, 2014). A related practice, moxibustion, involves burning herbs against the skin. Other practices, like placing animal feces over an umbilical cord, can cause unintentional harm. In these cases, families should be provided with education on the risks of this practice (Raman & Hodes, 2011). Additionally, Chinese or Sikh mothers are known to stay home for a 40-day period after childbirth in order to protect the child. This can result in missing two-week infant checkups but should be seen in context rather than considered medical neglect (Fontes, 2005).

Culturally diverse people can engage in spiritual or superstitious practices that are foreign to Westerners. People from Mediterranean or Middle Eastern cultures frequently carry an 'evil eye' amulet to ward off curses or bad energies. Latin American Catholic children may be given amulets of saints to wear on a necklace which they are not allowed to remove. Shia Muslim males can engage in a religious self-flagellation ceremony, leaving marks and bruises (Fontes, 2005). Haitian people often have strong belief in God, the Devil, and possession (Benedicty-Kokken, 2015). In these cultures, people with mental health, substance use problems, or legal problems are thought to be possessed by spirits or the Devil. For this reason, it is possible for Haitian parents to attempt to pray away demons in a bid to cure symptoms and behaviors. Again, while people are not homogenous within their cultures, it is important to consider cultural beliefs and practices when evaluating behaviors that seem foreign or odd to providers who primarily work from a more Western perspective.

CASE STUDY

Maria is an eight-year-old girl of Latina descent. Maria's parents, immigrants from Cuba and Mexico, sought counseling for Maria after she got in trouble at school for arguing with other children on the playground and stealing candy from a classmate. The counselor working with Maria discusses emotions and how to make different choices and asks how Maria's parents react when she gets in trouble at school. Maria responds, 'Mommy uses the chancla when I get in trouble.' Unfamiliar with this word, the counselor asks Maria to elaborate and Maria explains the chancla is a flip-flop sandal her mother uses to discipline her by either throwing it across the room at Maria, slamming it on the table in front of her, or spanking her rear with it. The counselor asks Maria how she feels about the chancla and Maria shrugs and says, 'I don't know. She uses it with me and my brother. It doesn't really bother us.' Neither the counselor nor Maria's teachers ever reported seeing marks or bruises on Maria. Upon doing some research, the counselor discovers that the chancla is a disciplinary tool in some Latino families (Vidal, 2014).

CASE STUDY DISCUSSION PROMPTS

1. Describe the possible harm caused by Maria's mother's disciplinary methods.
2. Explore the possible mitigating factors of cultural context.
3. Explain what conclusion the counselor should draw about the discipline Maria receives at home.

SUMMARY

This chapter defined the various forms of child maltreatment and the way maltreatment is understood and characterized by United States laws. Forms of maltreatment include physical abuse, psychological abuse, sexual abuse, neglect, and abandonment. The influence of culture was then presented, including a note on relativism and universalism, with descriptions of harmful and acceptable cultural practices.

REFERENCES

Amnesty International. (n.d.). *The horror of 'honor killings,' even in US.* www.amnestyusa.org/the-horror-of-honor-killings-even-in-us/

Barcellos, S., Carvalho, L., & Lleras-Muney, A. (2010). *Child gender and parental investments in India: Are boys and girls treated differently?* RAND Corporation. https://doi.org/10.7249/wr756

Basu, D., & de Jong, R. (2010). Son targeting fertility behavior: Some consequences and determinants. *Demography, 47*(2), 521–536. https://doi.org/10.1353/dem.0.0110

Behrens, K. G. (2014). Virginity testing in South Africa: A cultural concession taken too far? *South African Journal of Philosophy, 33*(2), 177–187. https://doi.org/10.1080/02580136.2014.912471

Benedicty-Kokken, A. M. (2015). *Spirit possession in French, Haitian, and vodou thought: An intellectual history.* Lexington Books.

Chabad. (n.d.) *The basics of the Upsherin: A boy's first haircut.* Chabad Organization.

Chen, Y., Li, H., & Meng, L. (2013). Prenatal sex selection and missing girls in China: Evidence from the diffusion of diagnostic ultrasound. *Journal of Human Resources, 48*(1), 36–70. https://doi.org/10.3368/jhr.48.1.36

Child Welfare Information Gateway. (2019). *Definitions of child abuse and neglect* [Report]. US Department of Health and Human Services, Children's Bureau.

Commission on Gender Equality. (2005). *Submission to the Select Committee on Social Services. Children's Bill.* https://static.pmg.org.za/docs/2005/051214kotze.htm

Dow, D. M. (2019). *Mothering while black: Boundaries and burdens of middle-class parenthood.* University of California Press.

Falicov, C. J. (1998). *Latino families in therapy: A guide to multicultural practice.* The Guilford Press.

Fontes, L. A. (2005). *Child abuse and culture: Working with diverse families.* The Guilford Press.

Fontes, L. A., Cruz, M., & Tabachnick, J. (2001). Views of child sexual abuse in two cultural communities: An exploratory study among African Americans and Latinos. *Child Maltreatment, 6*(2), 103–117. https://doi.org/10.1177/1077559501006002003

Fowers, B. J., & Richardson, F. C. (1996). Why is multiculturalism good? *American Psychologist, 51,* 609–621.

Gershoff, E. T., & Grogan-Kaylor, A. (2016). Race as a moderator of associations between spanking and child outcomes. *Family Relations, 65*(3), 490–501. https://doi.org/10.1111/fare.12205

Gharib, M. (2019). Why virginity tests are making news – In the US and Afghanistan. *National Public Radio,* December 6.

Glover, J., & Liebling, H. (2017). Persistence and resistance of harmful traditional practices (HTPs) perpetuated against girls in Africa and Asia. *Journal of International Women's Studies, 19*(2), 44–64.

Goodwin, J. (2003). *Price of honor: Muslim women lift the veil of silence on the Islamic world* (rev edn). Plume.

Hart, S. N., Brassard, M. R., Bingeli, N. J., & Davidson, H. A. (2002). Psychological maltreatment. In J. Myers, L. Berliner, J. Briere, J. C. Hendrix, C. Jenny, & T. Reid (Eds.), *The APSAC handbook on child maltreatment.* Sage Publications.

Jayachandran, S., & Kuziemko, I. (2011). Why do mothers breastfeed girls less than boys? Evidence and implications for child health in India. *The Quarterly Journal of Economics, 126*(3), 1485–1538. https://doi.org/10.1093/qje/qjr029

Kinnier, R. T., Dixon, A. L., Barratt, T. M., & Moyer, E. L. (2008). Should universalism trump cultural relativism in counseling? *Counseling and Values, 52,* 113–124.

Kolhatkar, G., & Berkowitz, C. (2014). Cultural considerations and child maltreatment. *Pediatric Clinics of North America, 61*(5), 1007–1022. https://doi.org/10.1016/j.pcl.2014.06.005

Landon, B. G., Waechter, R., Wolfe, R., & Orlando, L. (2017). Corporal punishment and physical discipline in the Caribbean: Human rights and cultural practices. *Caribbean Journal of Psychology, 9*(1), 7–23. https://doi.org/10.13140/RG.2.2.12185.88166

Mather, M., & Feldman-Jacobs, C. (2015). *Women and girls at risk of female genital mutilation/cutting in the United States.* Population Reference Bureau.

Mesman, J., Branger, M., Woudstra, M., Emmen, R., Asanjarani, F., Carcamo, R., Hsiao, C., Mels, C., Selcuk, B., Soares, I., van Ginkel, J., Wang, L., Yavuz, M., & Alink, L. (2020). Crossing boundaries: A pilot study of maternal attitudes about child maltreatment in nine countries. *Child Abuse & Neglect, 99*, 104257. https://doi.org/10.1016/j.chiabu.2019.104257

Msuya, N. (2019). Concept of culture relativism and women's rights in sub-Saharan Africa. *Journal of Asian and African Studies, 54*(8), 1145–1158. https://doi.org/10.1177/0021909619863085

Mwambene, L., & Mawodza, O. (2017). Children's rights and standards and child marriage in Malawi. *African Studies Quarterly, 17*(3), 21–43.

Orenstein, D. (2000). *Lifecycles: Jewish women on life passages and personal milestones* (2nd edn). Jewish Lights.

Oster, E. (2009). Proximate sources of population sex imbalance in India. *Demography, 46*(2), 325–339. https://doi.org/10.1353/dem.0.0055

Rachels, J., & Rachels, S. (2015). *The elements of moral philosophy* (8th edn). McGraw-Hill Education.

Raman, S., & Hodes, D. (2011). Cultural issues in child maltreatment. *Journal of Paediatrics and Child Health, 48*, 30–37.

Righthand, S., Kerr, B. B., & Drach, K. (2003). *Child maltreatment risk assessments: An evaluation guide.* Taylor & Francis.

Rogoff, B. (2003). *The cultural nature of human development.* Oxford University Press.

Sedlack, A. J., & Broadhurst, D. D. (1996). *Third national incidence study of child abuse and neglect.* United States Department of Health and Human Services.

South African Human Rights Commission. (n.d.). *Harmful social and cultural practices – Virginity testing? Children's bill B70-B2003. Submission to the select Committee on Social Services.* www.sahrc.org.za/home/21/files/30%20 SAHRC%20Submission%20on%20Childrens%20Bill%20-%20Virginity%20 Testing%20(Parl.)%20Oct%202005.pdf

Taylor, C. A., Hamvas, L., & Paris, R. (2011). Perceived instrumentality and normativeness of corporal punishment use among black mothers. *Family Relations, 60*(1), 60–72. https://doi.org/10.1111/j.1741-3729.2010.00633.x

United Nations International Children's Emergency Fund. (2014). *Ending child marriage: Progress and prospects.* https://data.unicef.org/resources/ ending-child-marriage-progress-and-prospects/

United Nations International Children's Emergency Fund. (2016). *Female genital mutilation/cutting: A global concern.* www.unicef.org/media/files/FGMC_2016_brochure_final_UNICEF_SPREAD.pdf

United Nations International Children's Emergency Fund. (2019). *Co-sleeping and SIDS: A guide for health professionals.* www.unicef.org.uk/babyfriendly/wp-content/uploads/sites/2/2016/07/Co-sleeping-and-SIDS-A-Guide-for-Health-Professionals.pdf

Vidal, J. (2014). 'La Chancla': Flip flops as a tool of discipline. *National Public Radio*, November 4.

World Health Organization. (2002). *World report on violence and health* [Report]. WHO.

World Health Organization. (2014). *Adolescent pregnancy factsheet.* WHO.

World Health Organization. (2020). *Female genital mutilation factsheet.* WHO.

CHAPTER THREE

Effects of Child Maltreatment

Children who experience maltreatment are prone to behavioral and emotional disturbances and a range of psychiatric disorders. Psychological effects and neuropsychological changes resulting from maltreatment can result in both short-term and long-term consequences, some of which can even affect physical health and medical outcomes. Not only do children suffer these effects themselves, often well into adulthood, they can also be prone to repeating cycles of abuse either through further victimization or by committing abusive acts themselves, as evidenced in the cycle of violence theory. Maltreatment also imposes a significant socioeconomic cost to individuals and society at large, and the intersection of cultural factors further complicates maltreatment and its effects. Providers must understand how maltreatment manifests physically, psychologically, and neurologically in order to accurately evaluate if maltreatment has occurred as well as how a child's environment may be affecting them.

TYPE I VS TYPE II TRAUMAS

Different kinds of traumas were categorized by Terr (1991) as either Type I or Type II traumas. Terr's Type I trauma refers to single-event trauma exposure. This means experiencing one traumatic event like an assault or being a victim of a crime. Terr's Type II trauma, on the other hand, refers to multiple traumas experienced over time or long-term chronic traumas. This can mean multiple instances of physical or sexual abuse over time, household violence or neglect that occurs over a long period of time, or poly-victimization – enduring multiple forms of abuse simultaneously. Children who experience Type II traumas are at greater risk of further trauma and victimization, development of psychological disorders, and both internalizing and externalizing behaviors (van der Kolk et al., 2019). Children who are abused and neglected are more likely to experience Type II traumas, as these incidents tend to be chronic and reoccurring, and are likely to experience multiple forms of abuse at once.

EFFECTS OF CHILD MALTREATMENT

Children who experience any sort of maltreatment are prone to a range of adverse effects, including symptoms that endure through the lifespan. Those who experience multiple types of maltreatment and chronic, longstanding maltreatment, are at even greater risk. These effects have been documented by researchers and clinicians spanning decades, and include emotional, cognitive, behavioral, psychological, and physical manifestations. Neuropsychological changes, as a result of maltreatment, have been observed in multiple studies, leading researchers to conclude that these changes in the developing brain might be responsible for both immediate and chronic responses to abuse and neglect.

NEUROPSYCHOLOGICAL EFFECTS

An array of neuropsychological changes are associated with experiencing child maltreatment. It is thought that because these changes affect the still-developing brain, they result in long-term effects that persist across the lifespan. Areas of the nervous system found to be affected by maltreatment include gray and white matter, the hypopituitary adrenal (HPA) axis, the hippocampus, the amygdala, and the corpus callosum (Gold et al., 2016; Hein & Monk, 2016; Kolb & Wishaw, 2015; Teicher et al., 2003; Yang et al., 2017). These changes in brain and nervous system structure and function are linked to acquisition of developmental disorders, and adverse influence on future relationships and experiences.

Changes associated with child maltreatment are seen in the functioning of the hypothalamic-pituitary-adrenal axis, the system responsible for activating and regulating the body's neurochemical stress response. Child abuse can lead to changes in dopamine and cortisol levels and these dysregulations are associated with cognitive decline, mental health disorders, and internalizing symptoms (Cabrera et al., 2020). The amygdala, responsible for processing emotional stimuli, can be larger or overactive in victims of childhood abuse and neglect, which can lead to heightened sensitivity to fear. Those with a hyperactive amygdala often detect danger and fear at higher rates (Hanson et al., 2010).

Child maltreatment has also been associated with changes in the hippocampus, a structure integral to learning, memory, emotional processes and other functions. Changes in the hippocampus result from physiological reactions to maltreatment that affect hormonal functioning. This dysregulation is associated with changes in learning and memory as well as increased predisposition to later development of posttraumatic stress disorder (Cabrera et al., 2020; Francati et al., 2007). Alterations in the structure and function of the corpus callosum and prefrontal cortex are associated with child maltreatment as well. In brains of maltreated children, the corpus callosum, responsible for facilitating communication between the left and right hemispheres of the brain, has shown decreased interaction between the brain hemispheres, which could lead to disrupted transfer of sensory-based information (Cabrera et al., 2020). The prefrontal cortex, responsible for executive functioning and higher-order thinking, can become hyperresponsive and create dysregulations in hormone and neurotransmitter function, leading to disrupted socioemotional processing (Cabrera et al., 2020). Finally, in children who experience dissociation, or a disruption in the continuity of consciousness, links between this experience and child maltreatment have been attributed to possible changes in specific binding protein genes (Yaylaci et al., 2016). The neurophysiological effects of maltreatment associated with brain and nervous structures are outlined in Table 3.1.

SHORT-TERM EFFECTS OF CHILD MALTREATMENT

Various immediate and short-term effects have been observed resulting from child maltreatment. For the purposes of this text, short-term effects are defined as problems that manifest within up to a few months subsequent to abuse and may persist through childhood. Long-term effects, on the other hand, are effects seen well into adulthood, often

Table 3.1 Brain and Nervous System Structures Affected by Child Maltreatment

Neurological Structure	Function	Child Maltreatment Effects	Resulting Manifestations
Hypothalamic-Pituitary-Adrenal Axis (HPA)	Regulating body's stress response	Dysregulated dopamine and cortisol release	Cognitive deficits Mental health disorders Internalizing symptoms
Amygdala	Processing emotional stimuli	Change in amygdala volume Hyperactivity in amygdala	Increased sensitivity to fear or perceived danger
Hippocampus	Learning Memory Emotion processing	Hormone and neurotransmitter dysregulation Ripple effect to HPA	Changes in learning and memory Increased predisposition to PTSD
Corpus Callosum	Facilitating communication between left and right brain hemispheres	Decreased communication between left and right brain hemispheres	Disrupted transfer of sensory-based information
Prefrontal Cortex	Executive functioning Higher-order thinking	Hormone and neurotransmitter dysregulation	Disrupted socioemotional processing

persisting through the lifespan. Short-term effects of child maltreatment can include physical injuries, emotional disturbances, cognitive disturbances, behavioral problems, attachment disorders, psychological disorders, and developmental trauma. Table 3.2 outlines the short-term effects of child maltreatment.

PHYSICAL INJURIES

Children can experience physical injuries from physical abuse, sexual abuse, or neglect. Injuries from physical abuse can include broken bones, lacerations, head injuries, soft tissue injuries, etc. Injuries from sexual

Table 3.2 Short-Term Effects of Child Maltreatment

Physical	Broken bones Lacerations Head injuries Soft tissue injuries Injuries to the genitals Sexually transmitted infections Malnutrition Sores and infections Worsening dental health Worsening medical conditions
Emotional	Internalizing symptoms Externalizing symptoms Aggression Depression Anxiety Emotional distress Peer relationship problems Self-injury Suicidality Shame Low self-esteem Negative evaluation of self Difficulty adjusting to social situations Difficulty coping Low motivation Emotional dysregulation Hypervigilance
Cognitive	Developmental deficits Decreased scores on intelligence tests Poorer academic performance Language delays Attention problems Concentration problems Less abstract thinking Memory disruptions Poorer processing abilities Poorer perceptual reasoning
Behavioral	Aggression Bed-wetting Antisocial behaviors Sexualized behavior Poor boundaries Disobedience Lying Fighting Destruction of property Relationship difficulties

Table 3.2 Cont.

	Dating violence Truancy Running away Delinquency Substance use
Mental Health Disorders	Anxiety Depression Posttraumatic stress disorder Conduct disorder Oppositional defiant disorder Substance use disorders Eating disorders Dissociative disorders Separation anxiety Reactive attachment disorder Disinhibited social engagement disorder Developmental trauma disorder

abuse can include injuries to the genitals or internal organs and sexually transmitted infections. Injuries from neglect can include medical issues from malnutrition, sores and infections from dirty diapers, and declining dental health or medical conditions from lack of care.

EMOTIONAL DISTURBANCES

Studies have noted the ill effects of child maltreatment on children's emotional health. Both internalizing symptoms, like depression, and externalizing symptoms, like aggression, have been documented at higher rates in children who experienced maltreatment than those who have not. These effects can lead to emotional disorders, peer relationship problems, self-injury, and suicidality (Righthand et al., 2003). Children who have been sexually abused are more likely to experience emotional distress, psychosomatic symptoms, anxiety, phobias, depression, anger, posttraumatic stress, negative self-evaluation, shame, and loss of self-worth (Righthand et al., 2003). Psychological abuse has been linked to lower self-esteem, a negative appraisal of the self, and difficulty adjusting to social situations. Children who have been exposed to intimate partner violence show higher rates of depression and anxiety than children who were not exposed to family violence. Children who have experienced neglect can exhibit sadness, lack of motivation, passivity, and difficulty coping (Righthand et al., 2003). Abused and neglected children are also more likely to experience emotional hyperarousal, act impulsively, lack insight, experience intrusive thoughts, and be more hypervigilant (Cabrera et al., 2020).

COGNITIVE DISTURBANCES

Children who have been abused or neglected often have greater incidence of developmental deficits than children who were not abused or neglected. Some maltreated children have displayed decreased scores on intelligence tests than children who were not maltreated (Perez & Widom, 1994). Psychological abuse is correlated with poorer academic performance. Children who have been neglected are more likely to display delays in language, intellectual development, and academic achievement (Perez & Widom, 1994). Children who were referred for sexual abuse investigations displayed intellectual impairment and poor academic achievement (Jones et al., 2004). In another study, children who had been sexually abused scored lowest on IQ scores when compared to not only non-abused children, but also to children who had been physically abused but not sexually abused (Sadeh et al., 1994). Children diagnosed with maltreatment-related posttraumatic stress disorder have demonstrated poor functioning on assessments of attention, executive functioning, concentration tasks, abstract thinking, and memory (Beers & De Bellis, 2002; De Bellis, 2005; Porter et al., 2005). Further studies indicate that maltreated children demonstrate poorer processing abilities, language performance, and perceptual reasoning (De Bellis et al., 2009; De Bellis et al., 2013).

BEHAVIORAL PROBLEMS

Children who are victims of abuse and neglect are also at greater risk for behavioral problems and disorders. Children who have been sexually abused display higher rates of bed-wetting and antisocial behaviors (Righthand et al., 2003). Sexually abused children are also prone to sexualized behavior whether through having disinhibited boundaries or recreating sexual experiences alone or with other children. Psychological abuse is linked to higher rates of delinquency, aggressive behavior, and social problems. Children exposed to intimate partner violence display increased behavioral problems including disobedience, lying, fighting, destruction of property, relationship difficulties, and dating violence (O'Keefe, 1997; Righthand et al., 2003). Abusive or erratic parenting is associated with problems in adolescence, including poor engagement in academics, running away, and participation in delinquent activities (Tyler et al., 2007).

MENTAL HEALTH DIAGNOSES

Maltreated children display higher incidence of internalizing disorders, like anxiety and depression, and externalizing disorders like conduct disorder. Cumulative exposure to violence has been associated with increased incidence of externalizing behaviors. Child maltreatment is estimated to account for 45% of the population's attributable risk for childhood psychiatric disorders (Green et al., 2010). About 25% of children receiving outpatient mental health treatment for multiple psychiatric diagnoses report abuse and neglect histories (Ford et al., 2011). Children who have been sexually abused are diagnosed with substance use disorders, eating disorders, dissociative disorders, depression, and anxiety at higher rates than children who were not abused. Additionally, children with abuse and neglect histories are more likely to display symptoms of posttraumatic stress disorder, attachment disorders, and conduct disorders.

ATTACHMENT DISORDERS

Attachment disorders occur when children become insecurely attached to caregivers. Bowlby (1969) documented effects of secure and insecure attachment. Securely attached children find what Bowlby referred to as a secure base from their caregivers, meaning they feel confident to explore their surroundings while periodically returning to their caregivers for support, comfort, and reassurance. Insecurely attached children do not find comfort and security from their caregivers. They can display an array of responses to their caregivers. Children with insecure ambivalent attachment can vacillate between anger and comfort seeking behavior. Children with insecure avoidant attachment will avoid caregivers and not seek comfort, while children with insecure disorganized attachment can exhibit several of these behaviors (Ainsworth et al., 1978). Secure attachment is formed when caregivers consistently and appropriately respond to infants' needs while insecure attachment is formed when caregivers fail to respond or respond erratically to infants' needs. Children who have parents whose parenting styles are frightening, distant, or erratic are more likely to be insecurely attached (Juan et al., 2017).

Insecure attachment can lead to a number of negative emotional and behavioral consequences that persist through the lifespan and, in childhood, it can lead to attachment disorders. Reactive attachment disorder is characterized by a child not seeking or responding to comfort when distressed, emotionally withdrawn behavior lacking social responsiveness, fits of irritability, sadness, or fearfulness (American Psychiatric Association, 2013). A second disorder resulting from insecure attachment, disinhibited social engagement disorder, is characterized by a child indiscriminately approaching adult strangers, behaving in an overly familiar way with strangers, willingness to go with an adult stranger, and failure to check back in with caregivers in new settings (American Psychiatric Association, 2013).

DEVELOPMENTAL TRAUMA DISORDER

Many researchers and clinicians argue that the current trauma diagnosis of posttraumatic stress disorder (PTSD) is insufficient for addressing victims of Type II traumas or trauma that occurred during childhood.

Children who experience abuse and neglect are more likely to experience multiple traumas, multiple forms of abuse, and more chronic traumas. Yet, though these children often receive multiple psychiatric diagnoses, fewer than 5% are diagnosed with PTSD (D'Andrea et al., 2012). Researchers believe that this is attributed to the variance in symptoms caused by chronic and multiple traumas on the developing brain which do not align with the criteria for PTSD in the Diagnostic and Statistical Manual-5 (DSM-5). A new diagnosis of developmental trauma disorder (DTD) (van der Kolk, 2005) was proposed to accommodate children displaying these symptoms. DTD includes 15 symptoms across three biopsychosocial domains – emotion and somatic, cognition and behavior, and self and relationships. Symptoms include problems with emotional regulation, cognitive distortions, and behavioral dysregulation. DTD was found to be comorbid with attention deficit hyperactivity disorder, separation anxiety disorder, oppositional defiant disorder, conduct disorder, and panic disorder (van der Kolk et al., 2019).

LONG-TERM EFFECTS OF CHILD MALTREATMENT

Long-term effects of child maltreatment are defined as those that begin in adulthood, begin in childhood and persist through adulthood, or persist through the lifespan. The effects of being abused and neglected as a child have been correlated with development of a number of psychological and physical symptoms in adulthood. Psychological manifestations associated with childhood abuse include depression, anxiety, posttraumatic stress, personality disorders, suicidality, and substance use problems. Physical manifestations are more difficult to pinpoint, but increases in somatic symptoms as well as increased prevalence of conditions like heart disease and chronic lung disease have been documented in adults abused as children. Additionally, adults who grew up witnessing violence are more likely to be victims or perpetrators of intimate partner violence, and those who were sexually abused have a greater likelihood of being revictimized in adulthood. Table 3.3 outlines the long-term effects of child maltreatment.

Table 3.3 Long-Term Effects of Child Maltreatment

Psychological Effects	Alcohol abuse
	Drug abuse
	Depression
	Suicide attempt
	Anxiety
	Posttraumatic stress disorder
	Complex posttraumatic stress disorder
	Panic disorder
	Sexual dysfunction
	Poorer executive functioning
	Poorer working memory
	Dissociative symptoms
	Personality disorders
Physical Effects	Headaches
	Migraines
	Heart disease
	Cancer
	Chronic lung disease
	Skeletal fractures
	Liver disease
	Sexually transmitted infections
Lifetime Implications	Increased likelihood of criminal behavior
	Increased likelihood of committing IPV
	Increased likelihood of revictimization and experiencing IPV

THE ADVERSE CHILDHOOD EXPERIENCES (ACE) STUDY

The Adverse Childhood Experiences (ACE) Study was a landmark research study conducted in a collaborative effort between the Center for Disease Control and the Kaiser Permanente medical system. For this study, researchers surveyed over 9,000 adults using the Adverse Childhood Experience (ACE) instrument to determine the relationship between childhood adversity and the incidence of psychological and physiological health risk factors in adulthood. The ACE instrument consists of 10 yes-or-no questions across seven domains that include psychological, physical, and sexual abuse, caregiver substance use problems and mental illness, and household partner violence or criminal behavior. Findings from the ACE study indicated that adults who had experienced even one or more adverse childhood experiences had an increased likelihood of being diagnosed with a psychiatric disorder or certain medical conditions, or attempting suicide (Felitti et al., 1998).

ADULT PSYCHOLOGICAL MANIFESTATIONS OF ADVERSE CHILDHOOD EXPERIENCES

As documented in the ACE study and confirmed in many other studies, adults who survived maltreatment as children are significantly more likely to experience mental health symptoms and be diagnosed with psychiatric disorders. For some, disorders first emerged in childhood and persisted into adulthood, and for others, disorders developed in adulthood. The original ACE study found adults with adverse childhood experiences had between four and 12 times increased risk for alcohol abuse, drug abuse, depression, and suicide attempts (Felitti et al., 1998). Adults who experienced child abuse are also more likely to be affected by posttraumatic stress disorder, anxiety, anger, and borderline personality disorder (Wilson & Newins, 2018). One study found adults who were abused as children were six times as likely to develop PTSD compared with adults who were not abused (Afifi et al., 2009).

Maltreatment survivors are also likely to display higher rates of anxiety sensitivity, which may be a factor in development of certain psychiatric disorders like social anxiety, panic disorder, substance use disorders, and agoraphobia. Anxiety sensitivity is the propensity to interpret physical sensations associated with anxiety, like shortness of breath, as harmful, resulting in a triggering of the fear response (Wilson & Newins, 2018). Adults who were sexually abused as children were also found to be more prone to sexual dysfunction, while women who had a history of sexual abuse displayed poorer executive functioning and working memory (Wilson et al., 2011). Additionally, maltreatment has been found to be a predictive factor in development of dissociative symptoms in adulthood, particularly in cases of more chronic abuse (Yaylaci et al., 2016).

A strong link exists between experiences of child maltreatment and development of personality disorders. Childhood maltreatment predicts increased incidence of all personality disorders and is associated with persistent maladaptive traits that typically present in personality disorders such as impulsivity, emotional reactivity, and poor coping mechanisms (Afifi et al., 2011; Glaser et al., 2006). People who experienced childhood trauma, particularly complex or Type II traumas, were specifically more likely to develop borderline personality disorder. Exposure to multiple forms of maltreatment was reported in 90% of clients with a diagnosis of borderline personality disorder (Brakemeier et al., 2018).

As in the case of developmental trauma disorder, the diagnosis of posttraumatic stress disorder does not adequately address the symptoms of people who experienced Type II traumas. A diagnosis of complex PTSD (CPTSD) was proposed for addition in the Diagnostic and Statistical Manual (van der Kolk et al., 2009). This proposed diagnosis addresses the nuanced symptoms that survivors of Type II traumas can experience, which encompass the traditional PTSD symptoms and three additional symptom clusters referred to as disturbances in self-organization. Symptoms include hyperactivation and deactivation of emotional responses, negative self-concept, negative self-evaluation, and disturbed relationships. Numerous studies have also documented the increased severity of psychiatric symptoms in those who report two or more adverse childhood experiences, as well as the link to comorbid disorders, including personality disorders, whose symptoms often overlap with those of CPTSD (van der Kolk et al., 2009).

ADULT PHYSICAL MANIFESTATIONS OF ADVERSE CHILDHOOD EXPERIENCES

Experiencing adverse childhood experiences was correlated with increased rates of physical ailments in adulthood. These include ischemic heart disease, cancer, chronic lung disease, skeletal fractures, liver disease, and sexually transmitted infections (Felitti et al., 1998). Adverse childhood experiences are linked to higher prevalence of headaches, headache disorders, and migraines in both children and adults (Mansuri et al., 2020).

Researchers pose several possible explanations for the links between adverse childhood experiences and rates of physical ailments in adulthood. Some speculate that the emotional effects of maltreatment lead people to make poor health choices, leading to more negative health outcomes. Maltreatment survivors were found to be more likely to smoke, have had 50 or more sexual partners, and engage in less physical activity than those who were not maltreated (Felitti et al., 1998). Yet, other studies that controlled for detrimental health behaviors still found increased incidence of medical conditions like heart disease and cancer in individuals who had been abused as children (Merrick et al., 2018). This led researchers to study the neurophysiological effects of child maltreatment and how they contribute to development of diseases, particularly through dysregulation of the HPA axis. It is thought that dysregulations in hormones like cortisol lead to stress-induced changes in cells in other parts of the body which, in turn, trigger the onset of physical ailments.

CYCLE OF VIOLENCE

Studies have also associated child maltreatment, particularly exposure to intimate partner violence (IPV) with further victimization and perpetration of IPV and dating violence in adolescence and adulthood (O'Keefe, 1997; Righthand et al., 2003). One study found that adults exposed to IPV as children were three times as likely to become perpetrators of IPV (Ehrensaft et al., 2003). According to Widom's (1989) Cycle of Violence study, children who are victims of abuse or witnesses to violence are more likely to later victimize others. This cycle can be attributed to a number of explanations. Adults who were abused as children can be more prone to anger and chronic aggression, placing them at an increased likelihood for perpetuating violence. Widom found that child abuse and neglect increased the likelihood that a youth would be arrested by 53% and the likelihood that an adult would be arrested by 38%. Additionally, all forms of maltreatment are linked to increased prevalence of substance use disorders, which is also a major contributing factor to IPV and criminality.

Children who are maltreated also fail to learn how to form meaningful relationships. They often exhibit some form of insecure attachment, leading to poor choice of partners and dysfunctional relationship patterns. This can place them at an increased risk of revictimization or perpetration of violence (O'Keefe, 1997). Additionally, social learning theory indicates that victims of child abuse and children who witness IPV learn violence and aggression through modeled behavior. In one of the first studies in this area, researchers demonstrated that children exposed to depictions of physical violence were more likely to enact physical violence in their play than those who were not (Bandura et al., 1961). Currie & Tekin (2012) found that adults who were abused as children showed double the probability of engaging in crime. Sexual abuse was found to have the largest positive correlation with crime and the probability of committing crimes increased with the severity of the maltreatment.

SOCIOECONOMIC COST OF CHILD MALTREATMENT

The Centers for Disease Control estimated the economic toll of fatal and non-fatal childhood maltreatment at $124 billion in the United States, with the lifetime cost for each victim of child maltreatment being $210,012 (Fang et al., 2012). Maltreatment's socioeconomic cost is manifested through increased mental health disorders, physiological diseases, delinquency, criminal behavior, intimate partner violence, substance use disorders, and further perpetration of maltreatment on future children. As maltreatment was found to increase the rate of violence in its survivors, crimes committed by these individuals take a toll on society. Increased rates of intimate partner violence in survivors of child abuse also affect mental health outcomes for adults and children.

Additionally, effects of maltreatment can be passed down, not only through hereditary links in psychiatric disorders, but also through the effects maltreatment has on subsequent parenting. Mothers who were exposed to maltreatment were found to have children with higher rates of internalizing and externalizing symptoms (Esteves et al., 2017). These findings could be attributed to harsher parenting styles in mothers who were abused themselves, problems with insecure attachment that keep mothers who were abused from bonding with their children, and the prevalence of depression and anxiety in mothers who were abused. Pels et al. (2015) refer to these learned methods of harsh and punitive parenting as spillover effects, as they affect subsequent generations. Higher instances of substance use disorders in adults abused as children leads to an increased strain on the mental health and medical systems as well as loss of life and opportunity for victims. The numerous lifelong consequences of child maltreatment add up to enormous costs in the mental health, medical, and legal systems and cost individuals their health, mental health, educational and vocational opportunities, healthy relationships, and sometimes their lives.

CULTURAL INTERSECTION

As discussed in Chapter 2, some researchers have wondered if the negative effects of certain acts, particularly physical discipline, are moderated by race and ethnicity. They pondered whether if physical discipline is an accepted form of discipline in certain cultures perhaps the ill effects often linked to it are decreased. Yet, in several studies physical punishment was related to adverse effects at similar rates for both children of color and white children and no beneficial effects were found to stem from physical punishment (Gershoff & Grogan-Kaylor, 2016). Children from different cultures and ethnicities were found to respond in similar ways to maltreatment. Researchers found that children in South Korea were just as likely to experience negative behavioral outcomes in relation to maltreatment as children in the US (Cho et al., 2017).

Children from diverse cultures and ethnicities can have an even more difficult experience following childhood maltreatment. Latinas and white women who survived childhood sexual abuse were found to have similar levels of self-blame and negative perceptions of their own victimization (Kellogg & Hoffman, 1995). In some cases, however, Latina survivors of child sexual abuse were more likely to express shame and self-blame and display emotional and behavioral problems than white or Black girls (Shaw et al., 2001).

Outcomes can also be worsened by immigrant and refugee status, community adversity, and lack of service utilization. Children can enter the United States illegally and as refugees, either accompanied by family or alone. Being an unaccompanied refugee minor was found to negatively impact development and mental health outcomes (von Werthern et al., 2019). African refugees were found to have increased prevalence of PTSD and CPTSD, especially if they had experienced human rights violations (Barbieri et al., 2019). Immigrant and refugee children are also often separated from their parents and families, a traumatic experience in itself, and immigrant families are more likely to be isolated, making abuse within those families less likely to be detected (Fontes, 2005).

Community adversity like poverty, prevalence of substance abuse, and violence can all place parents at a disadvantage and destabilize family units. Families can struggle to provide adequate care to children and be at higher risk for poor or hazardous parenting. Similarly, caregivers who utilize community services are less likely to mistreat their children while those who cannot access or fail to utilize services are at greater risk. People of color have been more likely to experience community adversity and less likely to utilize services. Inequitable distributions of power and systemic racism also affect families of color in their choice of neighborhood, access to education, and economic opportunities, adding the overall risk of maltreatment to children in these communities (Briggs et al., 2015).

CASE STUDY

Trey, an 11-year-old Latino student, meets with his school counselor after he had a physical altercation with another child at school. The other child took food from Trey's plate during lunch in the cafeteria and Trey responded by yelling in the other child's face and pushing him down. In the school counselor's office, Trey seems sad and upset. He says he did not mean to hurt the other child and that they are friends, but he was 'just trying to protect my stuff.' The school counselor is aware that Trey's family is of lower socioeconomic status and that Trey receives assistance through free school lunches. Trey appears thin but not malnourished. When asked where he learned to defend his things in that way, Trey says, 'That's how my mom and dad do it. If they don't like something, they get in the other one's face about it.' Trey states that sometimes his parents yell and push each other around.

CASE STUDY DISCUSSION PROMPTS

1. Explain what the school counselor can conclude about Trey's behavior given the context.
2. Describe how the school counselor could best respond to Trey in this situation.
3. Explain how the school counselor could determine if a report should be made to a child protective services agency.

SUMMARY

This chapter presented the effects of child maltreatment, both short-term and long-term. Neuropsychological effects of maltreatment and associated medical and mental health conditions were discussed. The cycle of violence and socioeconomic costs of maltreatment were outlined. Finally, cultural implications on the effects of maltreatment were presented.

REFERENCES

Afifi, T. O., Boman, J., Fleisher, W., & Sareen, J. (2009). The relationship between child abuse, parental divorce, and lifetime mental disorders and suicidality in a nationally representative adult sample. *Child Abuse & Neglect, 33*(3), 139–147. https://doi.org/10.1016/j.chiabu.2008.12.009

Afifi, T. O., Mather, A., Boman, J., Fleisher, W., Enns, M. W., MacMillan, H., & Sareen, J. (2011). Childhood adversity and personality disorders: Results from a nationally representative population-based study. *Journal of Psychiatric Research, 45*(6), 814–822. https://doi.org/10.1016/j.jpsychires.2010.11.008

Ainsworth, M. D., Belhar, M., Waters, E., & Wall, S. (1978). *Patterns of attachment: A psychological study of the strange situation.* Lawrence Erlbaum.

American Psychiatric Association. (2013). *Diagnostic and statistical manual of mental disorders* (5th edn). APA.

Bandura, A., Ross, D., & Ross, S. A. (1961). Transmission of aggression through imitation of aggressive models. *The Journal of Abnormal and Social Psychology, 63*(3), 575–582. https://doi.org/10.1037/h0045925

Barbieri, A., Visco-Comandini, F., Fegatelli, D., Schepisi, C., Russo, V., Calò, F., Dessì, A., Cannella, G., & Stellacci, A. (2019). Complex trauma, PTSD and complex PTSD in African refugees. *European Journal of Psychotraumatology, 10*(1), 1700621. https://doi.org/10.1080/20008198.2019.1700621

Beers, S. R., & De Bellis, M. D. (2002). Neuropsychological function in children with maltreatment-related posttraumatic stress disorder. *American Journal of Psychiatry, 159*(3), 483–486. https://doi.org/10.1176/appi.ajp.159.3.483

Bowlby, J. (1969). *Attachment and loss, vol. 1: Attachment.* Basic Books.

Brakemeier, E.-L., Dobias, J., Hertel, J., Bohus, M., Limberger, M. F., Schramm, E., Radtke, M., Frank, P., Padberg, F., Sabass, L., Jobst, A., Jacob, G. A., Struck, N., Zimmermann, J., & Normann, C. (2018). Childhood maltreatment in women with borderline personality disorder, chronic depression, and episodic depression, and in healthy controls. *Psychotherapy and Psychosomatics, 87*(1), 49–51. https://doi.org/10.1159/000484481

Briggs, H. E., Quinn, A., Orellana, E., & Miller, K. M. (2015). Community adversity and children's mental health: Moderating effects of caregiver service utilization and race on children's internalizing and externalizing problems. *Child and Adolescent Social Work Journal, 32*(6), 555–565. https://doi.org/ 10.1007/s10560-015-0395-3

Cabrera, C., Torres, H., & Harcourt, S. (2020). The neurological and neuropsychological effects of child maltreatment. *Aggression and Violent Behavior, 54*, 1–11. https://doi.org/10.1016/j.avb.2020.101408

Cho, Y., Atteraya, M., & Joo, H. (2017). The effects of child maltreatment on childhood behavior problems in South Korea: Findings from the fifth Korea child and youth panel survey. *Asia Pacific Journal of Social Work and Development, 28*(1), 39–55. https://doi.org/10.1080/02185385.2017.1401956

Currie, J., & Tekin, E. (2012). Understanding the cycle: Childhood maltreatment and future crime. *Journal of Human Resources, 47*(2), 509–549. https://doi. org/10.1353/jhr.2012.0017

D'Andrea, W., Ford, J., Stolbach, B., Spinazzola, J., & van der Kolk, B. A. (2012). Understanding interpersonal trauma in children: Why we need a developmentally appropriate trauma diagnosis. *American Journal of Orthopsychiatry, 82*(2), 187–200. https://doi.org/10.1111/ j.1939-0025.2012.01154.x

De Bellis, M. D. (2005). The psychobiology of neglect. *Child Maltreatment, 10*(2), 150–172. https://doi.org/10.1177/1077559505275116

De Bellis, M. D., Hooper, S. R., Spratt, E. G., & Woolley, D. P. (2009). Neuropsychological findings in childhood neglect and their relationships to pediatric PTSD. *Journal of the International Neuropsychological Society, 15*(6), 868–878. https://doi.org/10.1017/s1355617709990464

De Bellis, M. D., Woolley, D. P., & Hooper, S. R. (2013). Neuropsychological findings in pediatric maltreatment. *Child Maltreatment, 18*(3), 171–183. https://doi.org/10.1177/1077559513497420

Ehrensaft, M. K., Cohen, P., Brown, J., Smailes, E., Chen, H., & Johnson, J. G. (2003). Intergenerational transmission of partner violence: A 20-year prospective study. *Journal of Consulting and Clinical Psychology, 71*(4), 741– 753. https://doi.org/10.1037/0022-006x.71.4.741

Esteves, K., Gray, S. O., Theall, K. P., & Drury, S. S. (2017). Impact of physical abuse on internalizing behavior across generations. *Journal of Child and Family Studies, 26*(10), 2753–2761. https://doi.org/10.1007/s10826-017-0780-y

Fang, X., Brown, D. S., Florence, C. S., & Mercy, J. A. (2012). The economic burden of child maltreatment in the United States and implications for prevention. *Child Abuse & Neglect, 36*(2), 156–165. https://doi.org/10.1016/j.chiabu.2011.10.006

Felitti, V. J., Anda, R. F., Nordenberg, D., Williamson, D. F., Spitz, A. M., Edwards, V., Koss, M. P., & Marks, J. S. (1998). Relationship of childhood abuse and household dysfunction to many of the leading causes of death in adults. *American Journal of Preventive Medicine, 14*(4), 245–258. https://doi.org/10.1016/s0749-3797(98)00017-8

Fontes, L. A. (2005). *Child abuse and culture: Working with diverse families.* The Guilford Press.

Ford, J. D., Wasser, T., & Connor, D. F. (2011). Identifying and determining the symptom severity associated with polyvictimization among psychiatrically impaired children in the outpatient setting. *Child Maltreatment, 16*(3), 216–226. https://doi.org/10.1177/1077559511406109

Francati, V., Vermetten, E., & Bremner, J. (2007). Functional neuroimaging studies in posttraumatic stress disorder: Review of current methods and findings. *Depression and Anxiety, 24*(3), 202–218. https://doi.org/10.1002/da.20208

Gershoff, E. T., & Grogan-Kaylor, A. (2016). Race as a moderator of associations between spanking and child outcomes. *Family Relations, 65*(3), 490–501. https://doi.org/10.1111/fare.12205

Glaser, J. P., van Os, J., Portegijs, P. J., & Myin-Germeys, I. (2006). Childhood trauma and emotional reactivity to daily life stress in adult frequent attenders of general practitioners. *Journal of Psychosomatic Research, 61*(2), 229–236. https://doi.org/10.1016/j.jpsychores.2006.04.014

Gold, A. L., Sheridan, M. A., Peverill, M., Busso, D. S., Lambert, H. K., Alves, S., Pine, D. S., & McLaughlin, K. A. (2016). Childhood abuse and reduced cortical thickness in brain regions involved in emotional processing. *Journal of Child Psychology and Psychiatry, 57*(10), 1154–1164. https://doi.org/10.1111/jcpp.12630

Green, J., McLaughlin, K. A., Berglund, P. A., Gruber, M. J., Sampson, N. A., Zaslavsky, A. M., & Kessler, R. C. (2010). Childhood adversities and adult psychiatric disorders in the national comorbidity survey replication I. *Archives of General Psychiatry, 67*(2), 113–123. https://doi.org/10.1001/archgenpsychiatry.2009.186

Hanson, J. L., Chung, M. K., Avants, B. B., Shirtcliff, E. A., Gee, J. C., Davidson, R. J., & Pollak, S. D. (2010). Early stress is associated with alterations in the orbitofrontal cortex: A tensor-based morphometry investigation of brain structure and behavioral risk. *Journal of Neuroscience, 30*(22), 7466–7472. https://doi.org/10.1523/jneurosci.0859-10.2010

Hein, T. C., & Monk, C. S. (2016). Research review: Neural response to threat in children, adolescents, and adults after child maltreatment – a quantitative meta-analysis. *Journal of Child Psychology and Psychiatry, 58*(3), 222–230. https://doi.org/10.1111/jcpp.12651

Jones, D., Trudinger, P., & Crawford, M. (2004). Intelligence and achievement of children referred following sexual abuse. *Journal of Paediatrics and Child Health, 40*(8), 455–460. https://doi.org/10.1111/j.1440-1754.2004.00427.x

Juan, S. C., Washington, H. M., & Kurlychek, M. C. (2017). Breaking the intergenerational cycle: Partner violence, child–parent attachment, and children's aggressive behaviors. *Journal of Interpersonal Violence, 35*(5–6), 1158–1181. https://doi.org/10.1177/0886260517692996

Kellogg, N. D., & Hoffman, T. J. (1995). Unwanted and illegal sexual experiences in childhood and adolescence. *Child Abuse & Neglect, 19*(12), 1457–1468. https://doi.org/10.1016/0145-2134(95)00094-9

Kolb, B., & Wishaw, I. Q. (2015). Brain development and plasticity. In D. DeBonis & B. Brooks (Eds.), *Fundamentals of human neuropsychology* (7th edn). Worth Publishers.

Mansuri, F., Nash, M., Bakour, C., & Kip, K. (2020). Adverse childhood experiences (ACES) and headaches among children: A cross-sectional analysis. *Headache: The Journal of Head and Face Pain, 60*(4), 735–744. https://doi.org/10.1111/head.13773

Merrick, M. T., Ford, D. C., Ports, K. A., & Guinn, A. S. (2018). Prevalence of adverse childhood experiences from the 2011–2014 behavioral risk factor surveillance system in 23 states. *JAMA Pediatrics, 172*(11), 1038–1044. https://doi.org/10.1001/jamapediatrics.2018.2537

O'Keefe, M. (1997). Predictors of dating violence among high school students. *Journal of Interpersonal Violence, 12*(4), 546–568. https://doi.org/10.1177/088626097012004005

Pels, T., van Rooij, F., & Distelbrink, M. (2015). The impact of intimate partner violence (IPV) on parenting by mothers within an ethnically diverse population in the Netherlands. *Journal of Family Violence, 30*(8), 1055–1067. https://doi.org/10.1007/s10896-015-9746-2

Perez, C. M., & Widom, C. (1994). Childhood victimization and long-term intellectual and academic outcomes. *Child Abuse & Neglect, 18*(8), 617–633. https://doi.org/10.1016/0145-2134(94)90012-4

Porter, C., Lawson, J. S., & Bigler, E. D. (2005). Neurobehavioral sequelae of child sexual abuse. *Child Neuropsychology, 11*(2), 203–220. https://doi.org/10.1080/092970490911379

Righthand, S., Kerr, B. B., & Drach, K. (2003). *Child maltreatment risk assessments: An evaluation guide.* Taylor & Francis.

Sadeh, A., Hayden, R. M., McGuire, J. D., Sachs, H., & Civita, R. (1994). Somatic, cognitive and emotional characteristics of abused children in a psychiatric hospital. *Child Psychiatry and Human Development, 24*(3), 191–200. https://doi.org/10.1007/bf02353196

Shaw, J. A., Lewis, J. E., Loeb, A., Rosado, J., & Rodriguez, R. A. (2001). A comparison of Hispanic and African American sexually abused girls and their families. *Child Abuse & Neglect, 25*(10), 1363–1379. https://doi.org/10.1016/s0145-2134(01)00272-1

Teicher, M. H., Andersen, S. L., Polcari, A., Anderson, C. M., Navalta, C. P., & Kim, D. M. (2003). The neurobiological consequences of early stress and childhood maltreatment. *Neuroscience & Biobehavioral Reviews, 27*(1–2), 33–44. https://doi.org/10.1016/s0149-7634(03)00007-1

Terr, L. C. (1991). Childhood traumas: An outline and overview. *American Journal of Psychiatry, 148*(1), 10–20. https://doi.org/10.1176/ajp.148.1.10

Tyler, K. A., Johnson, K. A., & Brownridge, D. A. (2007). A longitudinal study of the effects of child maltreatment on later outcomes among high-risk adolescents. *Journal of Youth and Adolescence, 37*(5), 506–521. https://doi.org/10.1007/s10964-007-9250-y

van der Kolk, B. A. (2005). Developmental trauma disorder: Toward a rational diagnosis for children with complex trauma histories. *Psychiatric Annals, 35*(5), 401–408. https://doi.org/10.3928/00485713-20050501-06

van der Kolk, B. A., Pynoos, R. S., Cicchetti, D., Cloitre, M., D'Andrea, W., Ford, J. D., Lieberman, A. F., Putnam, F. W., Saxe, G., Spinazzola, J., Stolbach, B. C., & Teacher, M. (2009). *Proposal to include a developmental trauma disorder diagnosis for children and adolescents in DSM-V.* www.traumacenter.org/announcements/DTD_NCTSN_official_submission_to_DSM_V_Final_Version.pdf van der Kolk, B. A., Ford, J. D., & Spinazzola, J. (2019). Comorbidity of developmental trauma disorder (DTD) and post-traumatic stress disorder: Findings from the DTD field trial. *European Journal of Psychotraumatology, 10*(1), 1562841. https://doi.org/10.1080/20008198.2018.1562841

von Werthern, M., Grigorakis, G., & Vizard, E. (2019). The mental health and wellbeing of unaccompanied refugee minors (URMs). *Child Abuse & Neglect, 98*, 104146. https://doi.org/10.1016/j.chiabu.2019.104146

Widom, C. S. (1989). Does violence beget violence? A critical examination of the literature. *Psychological Bulletin, 106*(1), 3–28. https://doi.org/10.1037/0033-2909.106.1.3

Wilson, K. R., Hansen, D. J., & Li, M. (2011). The traumatic stress response in child maltreatment and resultant neuropsychological effects. *Aggression and Violent Behavior, 16*(2), 87–97. https://doi.org/10.1016/j.avb.2010.12.007

Wilson, L. C., & Newins, A. R. (2018). The indirect effect of child maltreatment severity on adult PTSD symptoms through anxiety sensitivity. *Journal of Child Sexual Abuse, 27*(6), 682–698. https://doi.org/10.1080/10538712.2018.1488333

Yang, S., Cheng, Y., Mo, Y., Bai, Y., Shen, Z., Liu, F., Li, N., Jiang, L., Chen, W., Lu, Y., Sun, X., & Xu, X. (2017). Childhood maltreatment is associated with gray matter volume abnormalities in patients with first-episode depression. *Psychiatry Research: Neuroimaging, 268*, 27–34. https://doi.org/10.1016/j.pscychresns.2017.07.005

Yaylaci, F., Cicchetti, D., Rogosch, F. A., Bulut, O., & Hetzel, S. R. (2016). The interactive effects of child maltreatment and the FK506 binding protein 5 gene (FKBP5) on dissociative symptoms in adolescence. *Development and Psychopathology, 29*(3), 1105–1117. https://doi.org/10.1017/s095457941600105x

CHAPTER FOUR

Families at Risk

What puts some families at higher risk for maltreating children than others? Certain family characteristics are more closely associated with increased risk for maltreatment while others are associated with decreased risk and greater resiliency. Families can possess a number of risk factors, like low income or living in a high crime neighborhood, but still be at minimal risk for maltreatment because protective factors often mitigate risk. Therefore, providers must evaluate both risk and protective factors to accurately assess families.

Providers must also weigh the number of risk and protective factors, as high risk typically results from an accumulation of risk factors. Furthermore, risk and protective factors are not stagnant but can change over time and depend on context like age of the children and availability of resources. Cultural concerns can act as both risk and protective factors. Providers should also consider that some risk factors might reflect societal problems, rather than individual or family problems. Identification of risk factors is not meant to stereotype or pathologize parents. For example, parental depression is strongly correlated with child maltreatment, but providers should refrain from jumping to the conclusion that all parents with depression are abusive or neglectful to their children. Risk and protective factors should be evaluated in terms of their effect on parent functioning.

FAMILY RISK FACTORS

Family risk factors are characteristics that increase the risk of potential harm to children within a family. These include parent, child, and environmental characteristics. Each risk factor increases risk of child maltreatment in families, but an accumulation of risk factors is more detrimental than individual risk factors alone. In addition to cumulative risk factors, the way family characteristics interact with each other can increase chance of risk. For example, low income and financial insecurity have been associated with increased risk of maltreatment. Parents who

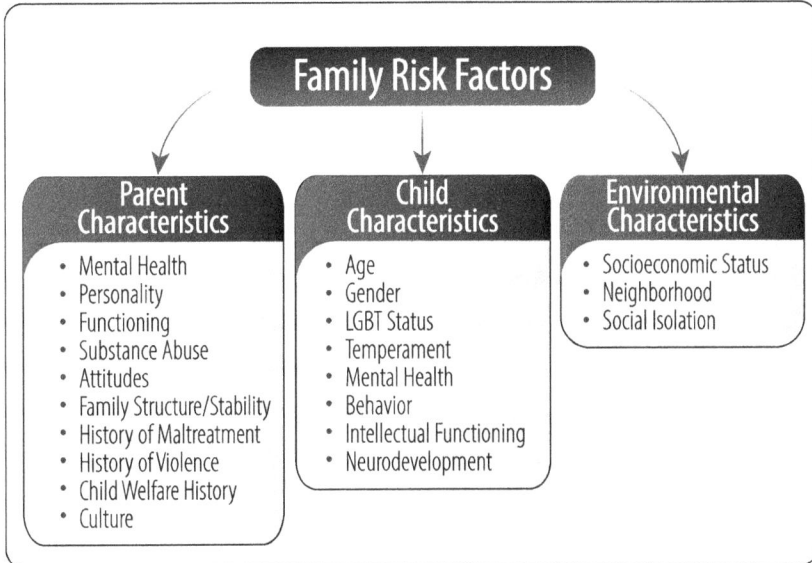

Figure 4.1 *Family Risk Factors*

struggle financially and also have substance use disorders can plunge themselves further into poverty, placing compounded stressors on the family, further predisposing any children to maltreatment. Some risk factors are more closely associated with certain forms of maltreatment. This is evident in the case of financial insecurity, which is strongly correlated with increased prevalence of neglect but not with sexual abuse, and intimate partner violence, which is more closely related to physical abuse than other forms of maltreatment (Brown et al., 1998). Figure 4.1 outlines family risk factors across parent, child, and environmental domains and Table 4.1 details these risk factors further.

PARENT CHARACTERISTICS

Parents can exhibit features that indicate they are at higher risk of maltreating their children. Some characteristics are more associated with a specific type of maltreatment, like physical abuse or neglect, while others increase risk for all forms of maltreatment. Parent characteristics

Table 4.1 Risk Factors for Child Maltreatment

Parent Characteristics	Low self-esteem
	Low self-efficacy
	External locus of control
	Developmental delays
	Low education level
	Substance use disorders
	Stress
	Anger
	Hyperreactivity
	Mental health problems
	Mental health disorders (depression, bipolar disorder, schizophrenia)
	Personality disorders
	Lack of empathy
	Apathy
	Domineering style
	Impulsivity
	Irresponsibility
	Poor social competence
	Poor problem solving skills
	Poor coping skills
	Cognitive inflexibility
	Parental stress
	Perception of child behaviors
	Ignorance of child development
	Disorganized families
	Unstable family structure
	Frequent moves
	Parental absence
	Parent history of child maltreatment
	Intimate partner violence
	Prior child welfare history
	Cultural factors
	Immigration status
Child Characteristics	Child age
	Premature birth
	Child gender
	Child sexual orientation
	Child temperament
	Child mental health
	Neurodevelopmental disorders (autism spectrum disorder, developmental delay, learning disability)

Table 4.1 Cont.

Environmental Characteristics	Economic insecurity
	Low income
	Poverty
	Unemployment
	Job insecurity
	Work stress
	Job loss
	Neighborhood disorder
	Neighborhood poverty
	Neighborhood violence
	Unstable housing
	Chaotic environments
	Community adversity
	Social isolation
	Lack of support

include mental health, personality, substance use, attitudes toward parenting, personal history of child maltreatment, history of domestic violence, history of criminal behavior, and cultural factors. Though child factors can influence maltreatment risk as well, parent factors were found to be the greatest contributors (Rijbroek et al., 2019).

PARENT MENTAL HEALTH

Parent mental health problems and low self-esteem are associated with increased risk for maltreatment (Rijbroek et al., 2019). Some of the factors most commonly associated with children being separated from their mothers are mental health problems, developmental delays, low education level, and substance use disorders (Milani et al., 2020). Parent mental health symptoms like anger, hyperreactivity, depression, and other psychopathologies were linked to child physical abuse in a meta-analysis of 155 studies (Stith et al., 2009). Depression is one of the strongest factors related to neglect and physical abuse. Depressed parents were found to be 3.45 times more likely to physically abuse children (Chaffin et al., 2001). Clinically depressed parents were also found to be more prone to behaving in a hostile and irritable way toward children (Silk et al., 2011).

Mental health disorders like schizophrenia and bipolar disorder have also been tied to higher rates of child physical abuse, particularly when these disorders are comorbid with substance use disorders or personality disorders (Goldberg & Blaauw, 2019). Stress, itself, can interact with other factors and predispose a parent to being more vulnerable to added risk factors or exacerbate other stressors. Family stress is specifically correlated to higher rates of harsh physical punishment (Koenig et al., 2000). Stress can be associated with major life changes, low income, or the perceived stress of being a parent. Other mental health symptoms associated with child maltreatment are hallucinations, delusions, paranoia, and grandiosity. Mental health factors pose the greatest risk when combined in context with other risk factors.

PARENT PERSONALITY AND FUNCTIONING

Certain parent personality traits have been linked to increased risk of child maltreatment. These include apathy, a domineering style, lack of empathy, external locus of control, impulsivity, hostility, low self-esteem, and sociopathy. Apathy has been associated with neglect while a domineering style is associated with physical abuse and intimate partner violence (Righthand et al., 2003). Lack of empathy has been correlated with intimate partner violence, physical abuse, and sexual violence.

Those with an external locus of control are at greater risk for neglect and physical abuse, perceiving themselves to be powerless in the face of stressors or child needs (Righthand et al., 2003). Parents who exhibit patterns of impulsive and irresponsible behavior have higher overall risk of abusing and neglecting children and those with hostile traits are at higher risk for physical abuse and neglect. Parents with low self-esteem can feel less competent when caring for children, yet parents with grandiose levels of self-esteem can be at higher risk for violence (Righthand et al., 2003).

Certain personality disorders have been linked to increased prevalence of abuse. Narcissistic parents were particularly prone to intimate partner violence and parents with antisocial personality disorder were found to be 25.7 times more likely to neglect their children (Swanson, 1994). Maternal sociopathy is associated with child physical abuse, sexual abuse, and neglect, and paternal sociopathy is associated with child neglect (Brown et al., 1998).

Parents with poor social competence and inadequate interpersonal skills can also be more likely to maltreat children. Poor social competence can lead to lack of social support or lack of ability to perceive and utilize sources of support. It can contribute to relationship instability and marital instability, two variables that have been associated with maltreatment (Righthand et al., 2003). Low intellectual functioning is correlated with physical abuse, sexual violence, and neglect. This factor is of particular concern when combined with other risk factors like lack of social support, medical problems, mental health disorders, or caring for multiple children (Righthand et al., 2003).

Other deficits like poor problem solving skills, poor abstract reasoning skills, cognitive inflexibility, and limited insight have all been linked to risk of child abuse and neglect. Parents with these deficits might have difficulty responding to children's needs and behaviors. Limited insight has been shown to impede emotional reasoning and the ability to differentiate child needs from parent needs. Parents with limited insight can perceive their children's behavior as more stressful than parents with greater insight and emotional capacity (Wolfe, 1999).

PARENT SUBSTANCE USE

Parental substance use disorders are identified as a significant risk factor for physical abuse and psychological abuse (Goldberg & Blaauw, 2019). Drug use has been associated with violence, aggression, intimate partner violence, and child maltreatment (Cafferky et al., 2018; Stith et al., 2009). Alcohol, however, is more closely linked to child physical abuse than is drug use (Stith et al., 2009). Substance use problems are often not the sole factor in families where children are maltreated. It is more damaging when combined with other factors like dangerous environment, personality disorders, and other mental health disorders.

PARENT ATTITUDES

Parents who abuse and neglect children display different interaction styles and attitudes toward children. They tend to expend less energy engaging children in activities that stimulate neurodevelopment and emotional development. They also provide fewer positive responses and praise, and less-clear instructions (Brown et al., 1998). Maltreating parents can also engage in inconsistent ways, respond negatively to prosocial child behaviors and reciprocate, rather than quell, children's disruptive behavior (Righthand et al., 2003). These parents are less flexible in their discipline and general response to children's behavior. Abusive parents can be more likely to attribute negative motives to other people's behavior, including their children's, and can have developmentally inappropriate expectations of children's needs and behaviors. Parents' uninformed and unreasonable expectations of children can lead them to feeling disappointed in and frustrated with their children, increasing the risk of maltreatment (Carr, 2013).

Child maltreatment is also strongly linked to negative maternal attitudes. These can stem from conditions like the pregnancy being unwanted or household stress, and are associated with abuse and neglect through a possible lack of bonding between mother and child (Brown et al., 1998). For both mothers and fathers, parenting stress, or the stress one experiences within the role of being a parent, is also correlated with increased prevalence of child maltreatment (Stith et al., 2009). Parents who abuse their children are more likely to rate parenting as stressful than non-abusive parents (Curenton et al., 2009). Parents who experience personal stress are also more likely to be overwhelmed by the stress of raising a child, particularly a child they perceive as challenging (Holden & Banez, 1996).

FAMILY STRUCTURE AND STABILITY

Younger parents are consistently found to be at greater risk for neglecting their children (Daniel et al., 2010). Single-parent households were found to be at greater risk for chronic neglect, as were larger families (Daniel et al., 2010). Families who exhibit child maltreatment are also more likely to have unstable or unpredictable family structures. These families lack flexibility in terms of individual roles. Communication in these families is not cooperative but coercive and combative (Tucker & Rodriguez, 2014). Homes with frequent changes in household members, frequent moves, or parental absences have been linked to child maltreatment. Parental absences have been specifically linked with interpersonal violence and partner violence (Righthand et al., 2003). Nonbiological parents were found to be at greater risk for physical and sexual abuse, though most abuse and neglect is committed by biological parents (Brown et al., 1998).

PARENT'S HISTORY OF MALTREATMENT

Parents who were abused or neglected as children, themselves, are at greater risk of maltreating their own children (Rijbroek et al., 2019), a phenomenon known as intergenerational transmission of maltreatment. One study found that 70% of parents who were maltreated as children went on to abuse and neglect their own children (Sroufe et al., 2005). Mothers who lived in out-of-home placements when they were children were at greater risk of committing maltreatment (Wall-Wieler et al., 2018). Parents who experienced poor nurturing or inadequate supervision in their own childhoods are also more likely to be abusive and neglectful as parents themselves (Righthand et al., 2003). This could be due to insecure attachment styles or modeled maladaptive parenting.

History of violence in the family-of-origin is another risk factor for intergenerational violence. Parents who experienced violent family interaction patterns are more likely to mistreat their families and be referred for abuse and neglect allegations (Righthand et al., 2003). One study found that parents with histories of neglect, physical abuse, or sexual abuse were more likely to have their parental rights terminated if they entered the child welfare system (Schetky et al., 1979). Similarly, parents who were exposed to psychological abuse or witnessed intimate partner abuse as children are more likely to perpetuate maltreatment with their own children. The original cycle of violence study found that 30% of children who experienced physical abuse went on to become parents who perpetuated child physical abuse (Widom, 1989).

PARENT'S HISTORY OF VIOLENCE

A history of violence both within and outside of the family is a risk factor for child maltreatment. Intimate partner violence is thought to increase the risk of child maltreatment through the psychological trauma of exposure to violence. Spillover effects can also link intimate partner violence to risk of child maltreatment as the quality of the marital relationship has been found to mirror the quality of parent-child relationships (Engfer, 1988). Intimate partner violence can also model aggression to children and other caregivers, which can spill into parent-child interactions. One study determined child maltreatment was present in 40% of intimate partner violence cases (Herrenkohl et al., 2008). Family violence has been associated with increased risk of child sexual abuse recurrence (Palusci & Ilardi, 2019), and 45% of mothers referred to child welfare agencies reported a history of intimate partner violence (Hazen et al., 2004).

History of violence against people outside of the family points to higher risk for maltreatment as well. Acts of criminal aggression, such as robbery, destruction of property, or violence against another individual, have been associated with increased incidence of family violence. Using weapons or threatening others with weapons has been associated with increased levels of intimate partner violence (Righthand et al., 2003).

PRIOR CHILD WELFARE HISTORY

Prior acts of abuse and neglect are associated with child maltreatment, having numerous referrals to child welfare agencies, intimate partner violence, and sexual offending (Righthand et al., 2003). In fact, history of prior child maltreatment reports is a significant predictive factor in future maltreatment reports. One study found that by age 12, 42% of children with one child protective services report had received a second report (Kim & Drake, 2019).

FAMILY CULTURAL FACTORS

Culture can be a risk factor in both increasing and concealing maltreatment. Ethnic and racial minority families are more likely to experience community adversity like financial insecurity, inequitable systems of power, racism, and oppression. Additionally, these families are more likely to experience residential segregation, underfunded school systems, economic insecurity, and reduced educational and vocational opportunities, all of which can place them at higher risk for child maltreatment (Alperstein & Raman, 2003; Briggs et al., 2015; Miller et al., 2010).

Cultural norms can interfere with disclosure and discovery of sexual abuse. This can be attributed to cultural values, household differences, and family structures. Latina girls who were sexually abused were found to be more likely to live with the perpetrator (Fontes & Plummer, 2010). They also experience more incidents of abuse and longer periods of nondisclosure, which could be related to patriarchal household structures (Fontes & Plummer, 2010). Cultural values of shame, taboo, modesty, virginity, honor, and patriarchy can impede reporting of child sexual abuse. Children can feel shame about sexual acts and families might be reticent to disclose child sexual abuse for fear of judgment from neighbors, family, and friends surrounding cultural and religious taboos.

Some cultures can view sex as shameful for girls and pride female virginity, making people less likely to disclose sexual abuse to authorities. In patriarchal cultures, a girl's report might be deemed as having little merit. Males are expected to dominate family structures in patriarchal cultures, thus impeding disclosure and possibly excusing abuse (Fontes & Plummer, 2010). People who descend from collectivistic cultures might also be more hesitant to disclose child sexual abuse, or fail to report abuse, in order to spare the family the perceived shame associated with child sexual abuse, particularly if the abuse occurred between a same-sex victim and perpetrator (Back et al., 2003).

Immigrant children and children from immigrant households can be at a greater risk of being maltreated (Alink et al., 2013). In a study of Korean immigrant parents, immigrant parental stress predicted risk of child maltreatment more than any other risk factors. Immigrant parental stress was also the strongest predictor of psychological abuse and physical neglect (Yoo, 2019). While parental stress is a risk factor for all families, immigrant parents can experience a different form of parental stress. Their stress can be compounded by acculturative stress, acculturation differences between parents and children, increased marital conflict, financial difficulties, and a lack of social support and resources (Yoo, 2019).

Immigrant families face a myriad of challenges. They might grapple with extreme cultural differences between their culture of origin and the dominant culture. Immigrants can be the target of discrimination and experience anxiety when interacting with nonimmigrants in their daily lives. This can lead to a sense of paranoia in immigrant families struggling to know who can be trusted (Fontes, 2005). Immigrant parents might have endured ethnic violence or conflict and can have symptoms of posttraumatic stress. These experiences can worsen the isolation many immigrant families already experience. Additionally, immigrants might be refugees and may have had to leave their loved ones behind, leaving them with little social support in their new homes.

CHILD CHARACTERISTICS

Various child characteristics can place some children at greater risk for abuse and neglect. Typically, these are not factors that children can control. For example, children with physical disabilities and medical conditions are at greater risk of fatal child maltreatment (Douglas, 2016). Child characteristics that increase risk for maltreatment include child age, child gender, LGBTQ status, child temperament, mental health, and neurodevelopmental disorders.

CHILD AGE

Rates of child maltreatment vary by child age group, with older children being more likely to be maltreated but younger children more likely to suffer fatal maltreatment. Younger children, particularly infants, are at greatest risk for fatal child maltreatment. Around 50% of child maltreatment fatalities involve children under the age of one and nearly 75% involve children under the age of four (US Department of Health & Human Services, 2017).

Non-fatal maltreatment rates increase during middle childhood. Physical abuse and neglect are observed most often in children aged 6–11, and are less seen in infants, toddlers, and adolescents. Sexual abuse rates increase after age three (Sedlack & Broadhurst, 1996). Children who were born prematurely were found to be at greater risk for maltreatment, as well as children younger than five years old (Rijbroek et al., 2019). Earlier onset of maltreatment is usually linked to poorer outcomes and multiple referrals to child welfare agencies (Rijbroek et al., 2019).

CHILD GENDER

Rates of maltreatment can vary by gender. Female gender was particularly associated with risk of recurrence of child sexual abuse (Palusci & Ilardi, 2019) and risk of sexual abuse overall (Sedlack & Broadhurst, 1996). Boys can have a greater risk of serious physical injury, physical neglect, and emotional neglect than girls. One study found physical abuse to be higher among male children (28.2%) than female children (16.7%) (Salem et al., 2020).

LGBTQ STATUS

Children who display same-sex interest, are transgender, or are gender nonconforming can face greater risk of maltreatment. In retrospective accounts, gay and bisexual men reported experiencing higher rates of child physical and psychological abuse by their mothers and major physical abuse by their fathers as compared to heterosexual men (Corliss et al., 2002). Lesbian and bisexual women reported experiencing higher rates of child physical abuse by both their mothers and fathers as compared to heterosexual women (Corliss et al., 2002). Higher prevalence of child sexual abuse has also been noted among LGBTQ youth as compared to non-LGBTQ youth (Austin et al., 2008; Balsam et al., 2005; Friedman et al., 2011).

CHILD TEMPERAMENT, MENTAL HEALTH, AND NEURODEVELOPMENT

Children with behavioral problems or difficult temperaments can be at greater risk for maltreatment (Afifi & MacMillan, 2011; Kim & Cicchetti, 2003). Children with emotional and behavioral challenges were found to be victims of chronic physical neglect at higher rates (Fluke et al., 2008). Children with neurodevelopmental disorders like autism spectrum disorder, learning disabilities, or intellectual disability are also at greater risk for maltreatment (McDonnell et al., 2019). One study found that children diagnosed with autism spectrum disorder and intellectual disability were up to three times as likely to experience all forms of maltreatment. Those diagnosed with comorbid autism and intellectual disability were at greater risk of experiencing physical abuse and neglect. Those with autism or intellectual disability, but no overlapping disorders, not only experienced higher rates of physical abuse and neglect, but were also victimized by more perpetrators compared to maltreated children without neurodevelopmental disorders (McDonnell et al., 2019). Being a victim of maltreatment was correlated with increased aggression, hyperactivity, and emotional dysregulation for children with autism spectrum disorder (McDonnell et al., 2019). Children with disabilities can be more vulnerable to injury and less able to defend themselves. They can also be more demanding, testing the limits of parents' internal and external resources.

ENVIRONMENTAL CHARACTERISTICS

Environmental characteristics refer to the family's ecology. Factors like socioeconomic status, employment status, neighborhood depression and social isolation are all risk factors for child maltreatment. For example, most child neglect cases tend to be clustered in low-income families (Righthand et al., 2003). Some environmental factors might be out of a family's control and should be considered in context.

SOCIOECONOMIC STATUS

Economic insecurity is correlated with physical harm (Yang & Maguire-Jack, 2018), financial instability is associated with fatal child maltreatment incidents (Douglas & Mohn, 2014), and financial insecurity has been correlated with reoccurrence of maltreatment reports (Kahn & Schwalbe, 2010). Financial insecurity has also been linked to higher rates of child neglect (Sedlack & Broadhurst, 1996). Parental unemployment was specifically found to be correlated with increased prevalence of physical abuse (Stith et al., 2009). Low income has been linked to lower parental sensitivity toward children and insecure-disorganized attachment patterns (Bakermans-Kranenburg et al., 2004; Cyr et al., 2010). Employment problems, unemployment, job insecurity, work stress, and employment termination have all been linked to child maltreatment (Fryer & Miyoshi, 1996; Wolfe, 1999).

Still, some researchers remind providers not to overlook possibilities for abuse and neglect in more affluent families. Abuse and neglect of children from affluent families is more likely to go undetected because of the lack of visible manifestations. Affluent families also tend to be less suspected of abuse and neglect by workers and are able to use their privileges and resources to resist and avoid intervention (Bernard, 2018; Felitti et al., 1998). Affluent families can have higher rates of neglect, particularly emotional neglect, that go undetected.

NEIGHBORHOOD RISK FACTORS

Neighborhood risk factors like disorder, poverty, and violence are correlated with increased risk for maltreatment. Neighborhood disorder and neighborhood poverty have both been linked to increased risk of chronic child neglect and physical abuse (Drake & Pandey, 1996; Guterman et al., 2009). Unstable housing and chaotic environments are most closely linked to chronic neglect (Logan-Greene & Semanchin Jones, 2017). Residential instability is also associated with maltreatment (Rijbroek et al., 2019). Families might have unstable housing arrangements or can become increasingly isolated if they are forced to move often.

Neighborhood conditions can also affect access to services and public assistance as well as rates of racial disparity (Landers et al., 2019). Community adversity can cause destabilization in families and impede parents' ability to provide supervision and nurturing of children. Parents experiencing community adversity report higher rates of psychological distress, mental health symptoms, and substance use problems (Briggs et al., 2015). Additionally, in many unsafe neighborhoods, children are often forced to stay inside where they may be more in the way of harmful adults. There may be more opportunity for discipline from parents, which can turn violent, particularly under stressful conditions (Fontes, 2005).

SOCIAL ISOLATION

Social isolation has been identified as one of the greatest environmental risk factors for child maltreatment (Carr, 2013). Social isolation constitutes a lack of material, social, and emotional resources. Parents who maltreat their children often state they feel disconnected from all major sources of support (Gracia & Musitu, 2003). The size of a parent's social network has been shown to moderate the relationship between experience of stress and number of abuse reports (Annerbäck et al., 2009). Parents who lack social support have fewer opportunities for emotional support, working through negative cognitions, positive reinforcement, and collaboration on parenting practices.

FAMILY PROTECTIVE FACTORS

Protective factors reduce the risk of maltreatment and the risk of maltreatment recurrence. Protective factors can be individual traits, family resources, and external support and services. Parent characteristics, child characteristics, and environmental or contextual factors can all decrease the risk of child maltreatment. Protective factors can combat the negative effects of some risk factors. Table 4.2 outlines protective factors for child maltreatment.

PARENT CHARACTERISTICS

Parents can exhibit personal traits and abilities that serve as protective factors against maltreatment. Parents who have better self-esteem and an internal locus of control are able to navigate interactions and solve problems more adeptly (Carr, 2013). Parents who are securely attached to their children are more likely to offer stability, consistent parenting, and positive feedback. Those who are willing to understand problems, accept help, and change their behavior are more help seeking and cooperative (Carr, 2013). Empathy and an understanding of typical child development can help parents respond more appropriately to children's needs and behaviors. Parents who were maltreated themselves but have an understanding of their experiences are less likely to maltreat their own children (Carr, 2013).

Table 4.2 Protective Factors for Child Maltreatment

Parent Characteristics	Positive self-esteem Self-efficacy Internal locus of control Problem solving skills Coping skills Empathy Help seeking and accepting Motivation for change Understanding of child development Understanding personal history of maltreatment and developmental history Cultural factors

Child Characteristics*
*These characteristics protect against
  the negative effects of maltreatment,
  rather than occurrence of
  maltreatment
	Intelligence
	Positive self-esteem
	Social competence
	Easier temperament
	Positive coping
	Social support

Environmental Characteristics	Social support Financial assistance Meeting basic needs

FAMILY CULTURAL FACTORS

Culture can be a protective factor by promoting self-esteem, self-efficacy, social support, and family cohesion. People can find a sense of pride in their culture. Their unique cultural identity can connect them to their personal values and a cohesive sense of self, improving mood symptoms and other maltreatment risk factors. Immigrants and refugees can find a sense of accomplishment in having overcome obstacles and in being able to provide for their families in a new land. This self-efficacy can lead to improved confidence, internal locus of control, and problem solving skills, all of which are protective factors against maltreatment. In some cultures, families include extended family, increasing availability of social support – a protective factor. Culture can also bring families together with shared traditions, rituals, and values. Cultural or religious practices can give families an opportunity to interact in positive ways, leading to improved attachment and more stable family dynamics.

CHILD CHARACTERISTICS

Child characteristics are not as likely to be protective against maltreatment itself. Rather, they can be protective against the effects of maltreatment. Some children can have certain characteristics that make them more resilient to abuse and neglect than others. Children who are intelligent tend to be more resilient and those with higher self-esteem have lower psychosocial stress and improved social connections (Carr, 2013). Social competence was shown to improve resilience and reduce prevalence of internalizing symptoms (Kim & Cicchetti, 2003). Children with an easier temperament are also more likely to have better coping strategies and can create a social support network more easily. Social support was also found to reduce depression, anxiety, and anger in children (Carr, 2013).

ENVIRONMENTAL CHARACTERISTICS

Family context can provide many protective factors against maltreatment. Parents with social support and access to resources are better able to function in a caregiving role. Access to basic needs and economic resources has been associated with improved family functioning and better treatment outcomes for families.

SOCIAL SUPPORT

Social support is a protective factor for both child maltreatment and intimate partner violence. Individuals with effective social support networks tend to report better physical and mental health overall. Social support can also help alleviate depression, a major risk factor for abuse and neglect (Ridings et al., 2016). For victims of intimate partner violence, social support can help with isolation. Victims with social support perceive that help is available to them and show a more adaptive response to stress (Fortin et al., 2012). Social support can also encourage healthy communication and improved problem solving skills. Friends and relatives can share parenting techniques with each other, improving parenting practices. Sources of support can be an outlet for stress and emotional difficulties, allowing parents to cope with their emotions in an appropriate way. As friends and loved ones sympathize with one another, compliment each other, and encourage each other, support can improve self-esteem, confidence, and self-efficacy. These factors, particularly parental well-being and self-efficacy, were found to be protective factors against neglect (Logan-Greene & Semanchin Jones, 2017).

RESOURCES

Family resources can be a key protective factor against child maltreatment. Being able to meet one's own basic needs was linked to overall improvement in family intervention programs (Ridings et al., 2016). Financial assistance was found to be a protective factor against chronic neglect (Logan-Greene & Semanchin Jones, 2017). Public assistance programs that help families meet their basic needs are shown to be more effective at preventing child maltreatment than programs that do not provide this (Chaffin et al., 2001). Basic needs include housing, utilities (heat, running water), food, clothing, medical care, childcare, a job, children's education, a source of social support, an emergency fund, etc.

WEIGHING RISK AND PROTECTIVE FACTORS

The cumulative risk hypothesis states that the combined and compounded effects of risk should be examined, rather than looking solely at isolated events (Evans et al., 2013). Risk factors become more dangerous as they accumulate and interact with one another over time (Lamela & Figueiredo, 2015). One study found that families with five or more risk factors were at greater risk for child maltreatment than those with two or fewer risk factors (Yang & Maguire-Jack, 2018). Risk factors can also contribute to each other.

The seminal study on adverse childhood experiences showed that having one risk factor increased the likelihood of having additional risk factors (Felitti et al., 1998). Masten and Cicchetti (2016) write that the interplay of risk factors and protective factors fluctuates across the developmental timeline. Numerous factors can interact to moderate the effects of child maltreatment and risk factors. For example, peer victimization was shown to increase the likelihood that children who were maltreated will develop some form of future psychological symptoms or disorder (Sansen et al., 2014). All risk factors and protective factors should be evaluated within context. The number of risk factors and the way risk factors intensify each other's effects should be examined. Protective factors should be evaluated for their ability to offset risk. All the while, providers should keep in mind that larger environmental and societal factors can all contribute to risk.

CASE STUDY

A forensic mental health evaluator is tasked with completing a parenting evaluation for Denise, a 23-year-old Black mother of two. The evaluation was ordered by the local child welfare agency to evaluate for risk of future harm to the children, a two-year-old girl and a six-month-old girl. The family came into the care of the child welfare agency when the two-year-old child was found wandering outside the home while the mother was in the shower.

The evaluator finds that Denise is of above-average intelligence but is struggling to complete her nursing degree at a local college. Denise states she has had to leave class to pick up her children multiple times, resulting in failing grades. Denise reports she leaves her children with family members or at homes in the neighborhood that function as unlicensed daycare facilities. Because she cannot afford a licensed daycare or other form of childcare, Denise is limited in her ability to work and complete her education.

When asked about the children's father, Denise reports he left the family before the second child was born. She states he does not send her financial assistance but occasionally stops by with toys for the children. Since the child welfare agency became involved, Denise has been receiving help with baby clothes and formula and is on a waitlist for daycare assistance. Denise states her family and friends are a big source of emotional support and they are also eager to help her with the children whenever possible, though they are not always available due to work and school obligations. Denise refers to her children as 'a blessing' and states she wanted both pregnancies, even if her relationship with the father did not work out. In fact, she expresses relief at his absence because of several physical altercations that took place, including one incident in which the children's father struck her while she was pregnant. 'I am better off doing it without him,' she states. Denise and her children appear bonded and she displays positive, engaged interactions with them.

CASE STUDY DISCUSSION PROMPTS

1. List the risk factors for this family.
2. List the protective factors for this family.
3. Describe the family's level of risk for child maltreatment. How can risk be minimized?

SUMMARY

This chapter explored the various case characteristics that can increase risk of child maltreatment. Risk factors include parent characteristics, child characteristics, and environmental characteristics. Family protective factors were presented for the same domains. Suggestions for evaluating both risk and protective factors in context were discussed. Risk factors are more harmful when they accumulate but protective factors can decrease some of this risk. Both risk and protective factors should be evaluated in context and in terms of their interaction.

REFERENCES

Afifi, T. O., & MacMillan, H. L. (2011). Resilience following child maltreatment: A review of protective factors. *The Canadian Journal of Psychiatry*, *56*(5), 266–272. https://doi.org/10.1177/070674371105600505

Alink, L. A., Euser, S., van Izendoorn, M. H., & Bakermans-Kranenburg, M. J. (2013). Is elevated risk of child maltreatment in immigrant families associated with socioeconomic status? Evidence from three sources. *International Journal of Psychology*, *48*(2), 117–127. https://doi.org/10.1080/00207594.2012.734622

Alperstein, G., & Raman, S. (2003). Promoting mental health and emotional well-being among children and youth: A role for community child health? *Child: Care, Health and Development*, *29*(4), 269–274. https://doi.org/10.1046/j.1365-2214.2003.00341.x

Annerbäck, E. M., Svedin, C.-G., & Gustafsson, P. A. (2009). Characteristic features of severe child physical abuse – a multi-informant approach. *Journal of Family Violence*, *25*(2), 165–172. https://doi.org/10.1007/s10896-009-9280-1

Austin, S., Jun, H.-J., Jackson, B., Spiegelman, D., Rich-Edwards, J., Corliss, H. L., & Wright, R. J. (2008). Disparities in child abuse victimization in lesbian, bisexual, and heterosexual women in the nurses' health study. *Journal of Women's Health*, *17*(4), 597–606. https://doi.org/10.1089/jwh.2007.0450

Back, S. E., Jackson, J. L., Fitzgerald, M., Shaffer, A., Salstrom, S., & Osman, M. (2003). Child sexual and physical abuse among college students in Singapore and the United States. *Child Abuse & Neglect*, *27*(11), 1259–1275. https://doi.org/10.1016/j.chiabu.2003.06.001

Bakermans-Kranenburg, M. J., van Izendoorn, M. H., & Kroonenberg, P. M. (2004). Differences in attachment security between African American and white children: Ethnicity or socio-economic status? *Infant Behavior and Development*, *27*(3), 417–433. https://doi.org/10.1016/j.infbeh.2004.02.002

Balsam, K. F., Rothblum, E. D., & Beauchaine, T. P. (2005). Victimization over the life span: A comparison of lesbian, gay, bisexual, and heterosexual siblings. *Journal of Consulting and Clinical Psychology*, *73*(3), 477–487. https://doi.org/10.1037/0022-006x.73.3.477

Bernard, C. (2018). Recognizing and addressing child neglect in affluent families. *Child & Family Social Work*, *24*(2), 340–347. https://doi.org/10.1111/cfs.12619

Briggs, H. E., Quinn, A., Orellana, E., & Miller, K. M. (2015). Community adversity and children's mental health: Moderating effects of caregiver service utilization and race on children's internalizing and externalizing problems. *Child and Adolescent Social Work Journal*, *32*(6), 555–565. https://doi.org/10.1007/s10560-015-0395-3

Brown, J., Cohen, P., Johnson, J. G., & Salzinger, S. (1998). A longitudinal analysis of risk factors for child maltreatment: Findings of a 17-year prospective study of officially recorded and self-reported child abuse and neglect. *Child Abuse & Neglect*, *22*(11), 1065–1078. https://doi.org/10.1016/s0145-2134(98)00087-8

Cafferky, B. M., Mendez, M., Anderson, J. R., & Stith, S. M. (2018). Substance use and intimate partner violence: A meta-analytic review. *Psychology of Violence*, *8*(1), 110–131. https://doi.org/10.1037/vio0000074

Carr, A. (2013). *The handbook of child and adolescent clinical psychology: A contextual approach* (2nd edn). Taylor & Francis.

Chaffin, M., Bonner, B. L., & Hill, R. F. (2001). Family preservation and family support programs: Child maltreatment outcomes across client risk levels and program types. *Child Abuse & Neglect*, *25*(10), 1269–1289. https://doi.org/10.1016/s0145-2134(01)00275-7

Corliss, H. L., Cochran, S. D., & Mays, V. M. (2002). Reports of parental maltreatment during childhood in a United States population-based survey of homosexual, bisexual, and heterosexual adults. *Child Abuse & Neglect*, *26*(11), 1165–1178. https://doi.org/10.1016/s0145-2134(02)00385-x

Curenton, S. M., McWey, L. M., & Bolen, M. G. (2009). Distinguishing maltreating versus nonmaltreating at-risk families: Implications for foster care and early childhood education interventions. *Families in Society: The Journal of Contemporary Social Services*, *90*(2), 176–182. https://doi.org/10.1606/1044-3894.3871

Cyr, C., Euser, E. M., Bakermans-Kranenburg, M. J., & van Izendoorn, M. H. (2010). Attachment security and disorganization in maltreating and high-risk families: A series of meta-analyses. *Development and Psychopathology*, *22*(1), 87–108. https://doi.org/10.1017/s0954579409990289

Daniel, B., Taylor, J., & Scott, J. (2010). Recognition of neglect and early response: Overview of a systematic review of the literature. *Child & Family Social Work, 15*(2), 248–257. https://doi.org/10.1111/ j.1365-2206.2009.00670.x

Douglas, E. M. (2016). Testing if social services prevent fatal child maltreatment among a sample of children previously known to child protective services. *Child Maltreatment, 21*(3), 239–249. https://doi.org/10.1177/ 1077559516657890

Douglas, E. M., & Mohn, B. L. (2014). Fatal and non-fatal child maltreatment in the US: An analysis of child, caregiver, and service utilization with the national child abuse and neglect data set. *Child Abuse & Neglect, 38*(1), 42–51. https://doi.org/10.1016/j.chiabu.2013.10.022

Drake, B., & Pandey, S. (1996). Understanding the relationship between neighborhood poverty and specific types of child maltreatment. *Child Abuse & Neglect, 20*(11), 1003–1018. https://doi.org/10.1016/ 0145-2134(96)00091-9

Engfer, A. (1988). The interrelatedness of marriage and the mother-child relationship. In R. A. Hinde & J. Stevenson-Hinde (Eds.), *Relationships within families: Mutual influences*. Clarendon.

Evans, G. W., Li, D., & Whipple, S. (2013). Cumulative risk and child development. *Psychological Bulletin, 139*(6), 1342–1396. https://doi.org/ 10.1037/a0031808

Felitti, V. J., Anda, R. F., Nordenberg, D., Williamson, D. F., Spitz, A. M., Edwards, V., Koss, M. P., & Marks, J. S. (1998). Relationship of childhood abuse and household dysfunction to many of the leading causes of death in adults. *American Journal of Preventive Medicine, 14*(4), 245–258. https://doi.org/ 10.1016/s0749-3797(98)00017-8

Fluke, J. D., Shusterman, G. R., Hollinshead, D. M., & Yuan, Y. Y. T. (2008). Longitudinal analysis of repeated child abuse reporting and victimization: Multistate analysis of associated factors. *Child Maltreatment, 13*(1), 76–88. https://doi.org/10.1177/1077559507311517

Fontes, L. A. (2005). *Child abuse and culture: Working with diverse families*. The Guilford Press.

Fontes, L. A., & Plummer, C. (2010). Cultural issues in disclosures of child sexual abuse. *Journal of Child Sexual Abuse, 19*(5), 491–518. https://doi.org/10.1080/ 10538712.2010.512520

Fortin, I., Guay, S., Lavoie, V., Boisvert, J.-M., & Beaudry, M. (2012). Intimate partner violence and psychological distress among young couples: Analysis of the moderating effect of social support. *Journal of Family Violence, 27*(1), 63–73. https://doi.org/10.1007/s10896-011-9402-4

Friedman, M. S., Marshal, M. P., Guadamuz, T. E., Wei, C., Wong, C. F., Saewyc, E. M., & Stall, R. (2011). A meta-analysis of disparities in childhood sexual abuse, parental physical abuse, and peer victimization among sexual minority and sexual nonminority individuals. *American Journal of Public Health, 101*(8), 1481–1494. https://doi.org/10.2105/ajph.2009.190009

Fryer, G. E., & Miyoshi, T. J. (1996). The role of the environment in the etiology of child maltreatment. *Aggression and Violent Behavior, 1*(4), 317–326. https://doi.org/10.1016/s1359-1789(96)00009-2

Goldberg, A. E., & Blaauw, E. (2019). Parental substance use disorder and child abuse: Risk factors for child maltreatment? *Psychiatry, Psychology and Law, 26*(6), 959–969. https://doi.org/10.1080/13218719.2019.1664277

Gracia, E., & Musitu, G. (2003). Social isolation from communities and child maltreatment: A cross-cultural comparison. *Child Abuse & Neglect, 27*(2), 153–168. https://doi.org/10.1016/s0145-2134(02)00538-0

Guterman, N. B., Lee, S. J., Taylor, C. A., & Rathouz, P. J. (2009). Parental perceptions of neighborhood processes, stress, personal control, and risk for physical child abuse and neglect. *Child Abuse & Neglect, 33*(12), 897–906. https://doi.org/10.1016/j.chiabu.2009.09.008

Hazen, A. L., Connelly, C. D., Kelleher, K., Landsverk, J., & Barth, R. (2004). Intimate partner violence among female caregivers of children reported for child maltreatment. *Child Abuse & Neglect, 28*(3), 301–319. https://doi.org/10.1016/j.chiabu.2003.09.016

Herrenkohl, T. I., Sousa, C., Tajima, E. A., Herrenkohl, R. C., & Moylan, C. A. (2008). Intersection of child abuse and children's exposure to domestic violence. *Trauma, Violence, & Abuse, 9*(2), 84–99. https://doi.org/10.1177/1524838008314797

Holden, E., & Banez, G. A. (1996). Child abuse potential and parenting stress within maltreating families. *Journal of Family Violence, 11*(1), 1–12. https://doi.org/10.1007/bf02333337

Kahn, J. M., & Schwalbe, C. (2010). The timing to and risk factors associated with child welfare system recidivism at two decision-making points. *Children and Youth Services Review, 32*(7), 1035–1044. https://doi.org/10.1016/j.childyouth.2010.04.011

Kim, H., & Drake, B. (2019). Cumulative prevalence of onset and recurrence of child maltreatment reports. *Journal of the American Academy of Child & Adolescent Psychiatry, 58*(12), 1175–1183. https://doi.org/10.1016/j.jaac.2019.02.015

Kim, J., & Cicchetti, D. (2003). Social self-efficacy and behavior problems in maltreated and nonmaltreated children. *Journal of Clinical Child & Adolescent Psychology, 32*(1), 106–117. https://doi.org/10.1207/s15374424jccp3201_10

Koenig, A. L., Cicchetti, D., & Rogosch, F. A. (2000). Child compliance/noncompliance and maternal contributors to internalization in maltreating and nonmaltreating dyads. *Child Development, 71*(4), 1018–1032. https://doi.org/10.1111/1467-8624.00206

Lamela, D., & Figueiredo, B. (2015). A cumulative risk model of child physical maltreatment potential: Findings from a community-based study. *Journal of Interpersonal Violence, 33*(8), 1287–1305. https://doi.org/10.1177/0886260515615142

Landers, A. L., Carrese, D. H., & Spath, R. (2019). A decade in review of trends in social work literature: The link between poverty and child maltreatment in the United States. *Child Welfare, 97*(4), 65–96.

Logan-Greene, P., & Semanchin Jones, A. (2017). Predicting chronic neglect: Understanding risk and protective factors for CPS-involved families. *Child & Family Social Work, 23*(2), 264–272. https://doi.org/10.1111/cfs.12414

Masten, A. S., & Cicchetti, D. (2016). Resilience in development: Progress and transformation. *Development and Psychopathology, 4,* 271–333.

McDonnell, C. G., Boan, A. D., Bradley, C. C., Seay, K. D., Charles, J. M., & Carpenter, L. A. (2019). Child maltreatment in autism spectrum disorder and intellectual disability: Results from a population-based sample. *Journal of Child Psychology and Psychiatry, 60*(5), 576–584. https://doi.org/10.1111/jcpp.12993

Milani, L., Grumi, S., Camisasca, E., Miragoli, S., Traficante, D., & Di Blasio, P. (2020). Familial risk and protective factors affecting CPS professionals' child removal decision: A decision tree analysis study. *Children and Youth Services Review, 109,* 104687. https://doi.org/10.1016/j.childyouth.2019.104687

Miller, K. M., Gil-Kashiwabara, E., Briggs, H. E., & Hatcher, S. (2010). Contexts of race, ethnicity, and culture for children of incarcerated parents. In J. M. Eddy & J. Poehlmann (Eds.), *Children of incarcerated parents: A handbook for researchers and practitioners.* The Urban Institute Press.

Palusci, V. J., & Ilardi, M. (2019). Risk factors and services to reduce child sexual abuse recurrence. *Child Maltreatment, 25*(1), 106–116. https://doi.org/10.1177/1077559519848489

Ridings, L. E., Beasley, L. O., & Silovsky, J. F. (2016). Consideration of risk and protective factors for families at risk for child maltreatment: An intervention approach. *Journal of Family Violence, 32*(2), 179–188. https://doi.org/10.1007/s10896-016-9826-y

Righthand, S., Kerr, B. B., & Drach, K. (2003). *Child maltreatment risk assessments: An evaluation guide.* Taylor & Francis.

Rijbroek, B., Strating, M. M., Konijn, H. W., & Huijsman, R. (2019). Child protection cases, one size fits all? Cluster analyses of risk and protective factors. *Child Abuse & Neglect, 95,* 104068. https://doi.org/10.1016/j.chiabu.2019.104068

Salem, M., Dargham, S. R., Kamal, M., Eldeeb, N., Alyafei, K. A., Lynch, M. A., Mian, M., & Mahfoud, Z. R. (2020). Effect of gender on childhood maltreatment in the state of Qatar: Retrospective study. *Child Abuse & Neglect, 101,* 104314. https://doi.org/10.1016/j.chiabu.2019.104314

Sansen, L., Iffland, B., & Neuner, F. (2014). Peer victimization predicts psychological symptoms beyond the effects of child maltreatment. *Psychiatry Research, 220*(3), 1051–1058. https://doi.org/10.1016/j.psychres.2014.09.008

Schetky, D. H., Angell, R., Morrison, C. V., & Sack, W. H. (1979). Parents who fail: A study of 51 cases of termination of parental rights. *Journal of the American Academy of Child Psychiatry, 18*(2), 366–383. https://doi.org/10.1016/s0002-7138(09)61049-9

Sedlack, A. J., & Broadhurst, D. D. (1996). *Third national incidence study of child abuse and neglect.* United States Department of Health and Human Services.

Silk, J. S., Shaw, D. S., Prout, J. T., O'Rourke, F., Lane, T. J., & Kovacs, M. (2011). Socialization of emotion and offspring internalizing symptoms in mothers with childhood-onset depression. *Journal of Applied Developmental Psychology, 32*(3), 127–136. https://doi.org/10.1016/j.appdev.2011.02.001

Sroufe, L. A., Collins, W. A., Carlson, E., Egeland, B., & Carlson, E. A. (2005). *The development of the person: The Minnesota study of risk and adaptation from birth to adulthood.* Guilford Publications, Inc.

Stith, S. M., Liu, T., Davies, L., Boykin, E. L., Alder, M. C., Harris, J. M., Som, A., McPherson, M., & Dees, J. (2009). Risk factors in child maltreatment: A meta-analytic review of the literature. *Aggression and Violent Behavior, 14*(1), 13–29. https://doi.org/10.1016/j.avb.2006.03.006

Swanson, J. W. (1994). Mental disorder, substance abuse, and community violence: An epidemiological approach. In J. Monahan & H. J. Steadman (Eds.), *Violence and mental disorder: Developments in risk assessment.* University of Chicago Press.

Tucker, M. C., & Rodriguez, C. M. (2014). Family dysfunction and social isolation as moderators between stress and child physical abuse risk. *Journal of Family Violence, 29*(2), 175–186. https://doi.org/10.1007/s10896-013-9567-0

US Department of Health & Human Services. (2017). *Child maltreatment 2015: Reports from the States to the National Child abuse and Neglect Data Systems – National statistics on child abuse and neglect.* www.acf.hhs.gov/cb/resource/child-maltreatment-2017

Wall-Wieler, E., Almquist, Y., Liu, C., Vinnerljung, B., & Hjern, A. (2018). Intergenerational transmission of out-of-home care in Sweden: A population-based cohort study. *Child Abuse & Neglect, 83,* 42–51. https://doi.org/10.1016/j.chiabu.2018.07.007

Widom, C. S. (1989). Does violence beget violence? A critical examination of the literature. *Psychological Bulletin, 106*(1), 3–28. https://doi.org/10.1037/0033-2909.106.1.3

Wolfe, D. A. (1999). *Child abuse: Implications for child development and psychopathology (developmental clinical psychology and psychiatry)* (2nd edn). Sage Publications, Inc.

Yang, M. Y., & Maguire-Jack, K. (2018). Individual and cumulative risks for child abuse and neglect. *Family Relations, 67*(2), 287–301. https://doi.org/10.1111/fare.12310

Yoo, S. Y. (2019). The impact of immigrant parental stress on the risk of child maltreatment among Korean immigrant parents. *Journal of Child & Adolescent Trauma, 12*(1), 49–59. https://doi.org/10.1007/s40653-017-0173-9

CHAPTER FIVE

Assessing Families for Risk

Effective assessment requires data collection from multiple sources including parents, children, extended family members and caregivers, teachers, and other collateral sources. Different forms of assessment should be used with each family in order to obtain a more complete understanding of family functioning. Providers must obtain information about family risk and protective factors, as well as determine how these factors interact to influence risk for maltreatment. The bioecological model helps providers conceptualize the interplay of risk and protective factors within a cultural and societal context. Obstacles to assessment include ambiguity, quality of information sources, cultural factors, and the non-fixed nature of risk factors. Providers must evaluate parent, child, and environmental characteristics fairly and in context, using both standardized measures and their clinical judgment.

THE BIOECOLOGICAL MODEL

According to Bronfenbrenner's (1979) bioecological theory of human development, child development can be understood through the interplay of individual, family, and community factors. Bronfenbrenner's bioecological theory posits that development is affected by the interaction of several systems over time. These systems include the microsystem, the mesosystem, the exosystem, and the macrosystem. The microsystem represents factors in the child's immediate environment, including family, peers, schools, and other places and people the child interacts with daily. The mesosystem represents the connections between the different systems. This includes connections between parents and teachers, interactions between classmates, and relationships with friends' parents. The exosystem encompasses external and community factors. These include the parents' work environment, local governments, and the media. The macrosystem refers to larger social constructs like culture, laws, and values. Belsky (1980) pointed to the added influence of ontogenic factors, or factors within the individual child, like temperament and behavioral health.

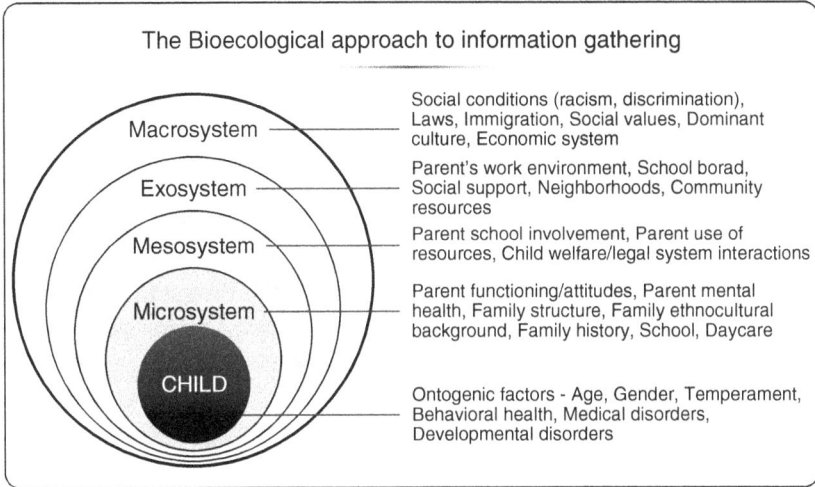

Figure 5.1 *The Bioecological Approach to Information Gathering*

Child maltreatment can be understood by examining the interplay of short-term and long-term factors across these developmental levels. Short-term events refer to immediate occurrences like job loss or moving homes, while long-term events refer to circumstances like low socio-economic status. Risk cannot be explained by any single factor alone. Providers must consider risk and protective factors across all developmental levels, as well as the mutual relationship between these factors (Cicchetti & Valentino, 2006). Figure 5.1 outlines the application of the bioecological approach to information gathering in child maltreatment risk assessment.

FORMS OF ASSESSMENT

Several forms of assessment are detailed in the family evaluation literature. Sperry (2019) outlines qualitative assessments, standardized assessments, observational assessments, self-reports, and continuous assessment. For the purposes of child maltreatment risk assessment, standardized, observational, and self-report are the most commonly utilized components, though integrating qualitative and continuous assessment can help provide a more complete, holistic view of family functioning. Multiple modes of assessment should be used for each case in order to evaluate all relevant domains.

QUALITATIVE ASSESSMENT

Qualitative assessment involves using creative methods to evoke specific family qualities. These can include role plays, genograms, unstructured interviews, and family art projects (Sperry, 2019). Qualitative assessments are more flexible and allow for multiple voices in a family to be heard. They honor cultural considerations and help providers understand family values, stories, and meaning making (Sperry, 2019).

STANDARDIZED ASSESSMENT

Standardized assessment tools include structured tests and instruments. These assessments are normed through large studies and have high reliability and validity. Standardized instruments make assessment more consistent across families and populations. They include specific cutoffs for maladaptive parent behaviors, parent traits, and other risk factors (Sperry, 2019). While standardized methods are useful for accurately measuring certain characteristics, they can ignore or negatively interpret cultural factors when they are normed on populations that are not culturally diverse.

OBSERVATIONAL ASSESSMENT

Observational assessment involves observing behaviors and interactions between people. Observational assessment can use video recordings or one-way mirrors to improve accuracy (Sperry, 2019). These assessments typically involve instructing a family to complete a task or have a conversation and then observing the patterns and dynamics between family members. Observational assessments can give insight into parenting styles, discipline strategies, the quality of attachment, parent interaction patterns, marital instability, and family boundaries. Observational assessments can be more inclusive of cultural differences than standardized assessments depending on the provider's cultural competence.

SELF-REPORT ASSESSMENT

Self-report assessments allow family members to report first-hand accounts of what transpires within the family. Brief paper-and-pencil measures are often used to help individuals quantify their experiences and rate the characteristics of other family members. Self-report measures can be used to assess family members' perceptions of each other, family members' behavior, and personal emotions and experiences (Sperry, 2019). In child maltreatment risk assessment, self-report measures can assess parent mental health and substance use, discipline strategies, children's behavior, and marital stability.

CONTINUOUS ASSESSMENT

Continuous assessment involves assessment of families over time. Continuous assessment is typically utilized to monitor treatment outcomes and inform ongoing treatment decisions (Sperry, 2019). Continuous assessment is most useful in families that are receiving services or treatment like psychotherapy, parenting instruction, and targeted child services. This form of assessment gives providers insight into the family's motivation and ability to change, obstacles to change, and other services that might need to be provided (Sperry, 2019).

CONSENSUS-BASED VS ACTUARIAL ASSESSMENT

As noted in Chapter 1, the merits of consensus-based and actuarial assessment models are widely debated. Consensus-based models rely on providers' clinical judgment. In these models, providers compare facts from a case to characteristics the clinical community has noted are related to risk. The goal is to make predictions of risk according to a database of cumulative knowledge. On the other hand, actuarial-based systems use structured, standardized checklists and instruments. These instruments are normed on large samples, using data that researchers have identified as indicative of risk. Actuarial methods have greater reliability and validity than consensus-based methods (Stroud & Warren-Adamson, 2013).

Consensus-based assessment relies on clinical expertise and intuitive decision making while actuarial assessment relies on analytical decision making. In consensus-based assessment, providers must use their individual knowledge, representative of cumulative knowledge in the field, to recognize patterns associated with risk. While decision making using actuarial instruments has been found to be more accurate than consensus-based decision making alone, the use of clinical expertise is still important. Expertise acquired through experience working with families and conducting assessments can provide crucial information for the overall evaluation of risk. Accurate risk assessments incorporate both intuitive and analytical decision making.

SOURCES OF INFORMATION

Sources of information can include individuals within the family and collateral sources. Family refers to parents, children, and other caregivers. Collateral sources refers to extended family, friends, and others within the community. Extended family and family friends can provide valuable information about family functioning, discipline, and values. Family friends and neighbors can also report if they have ever suspected any abuse or neglect. Other caregivers, like daycare and aftercare workers, can give insight into children's behavior, parent behavior, or signs of maltreatment. Teachers, school administrators, and school counselors can offer valuable information about a child's level of functioning, behavior, signs of maltreatment, and socioeconomic status. Other members of the community who come into contact with the family can be sources of information as well, like sports coaches, medical providers, mental health providers, and clergy.

For observational assessments, the provider can observe child behavior, parent-child behavior, family behavior, and parent interaction. Standardized tests can be given to children and parents to assess intelligence, personality, and mental health factors. Self-report instruments can be utilized with parents, children, and collateral sources. Qualitative assessments can be used with parents, children, and other family members. Providers must also obtain official records. Records can include school records, police reports, past child maltreatment reports, and medical and mental health records.

OBSTACLES TO ASSESSMENT

A number of obstacles can impede the assessment process. To begin with, risk assessment is differentiated from risk prediction. Violence is very difficult to predict, and studies found empirical methods for predicting violence typically fail (Righthand et al., 2003). Because prediction is not possible, risk assessment is the preferred strategy. This means, however, that risk factors can only be assessed and weighed against protective factors, not that violence or maltreatment can be predicted to occur or not occur.

Human development is a complex process and represents an interplay of fluctuating personal, situational, and environmental factors. As demonstrated in the bioecological model, numerous systems, and the connections between them, affect child development as well as family risk. Providers can focus on too few variables or fixate on single points in a timeline, decreasing the accuracy of their assessment (Righthand et al., 2003). Additionally, many of the known risk factors can point to some forms of maltreatment but not others, or cross over categories of maltreatment. Sexual abuse cases, in particular, can often have ambiguous signs. Children can be coerced into being silent or recant prior allegations out of fear or loyalty to the family. Children can also be easily suggestible and give false accounts based on leading questions. Many providers are not adequately trained in forensic interviewing strategies designed to withdraw information while minimizing suggestibility (Levenson & Morin, 2006).

Culture can also be an obstacle to assessment. Families from certain cultures, and immigrant families, can be suspicious of the system and hesitant to let in an observer, making it more challenging to obtain information. Providers can be ill-informed of cultural practices and beliefs, labeling behaviors as abusive when they might be culturally acceptable. Providers must also be conscious of not reproducing damaging methods and ideas from the social sciences' history of colonizing, Western-centric schemas. The values and traditions of Western whites are not to be seen as the standard while other cultures remain a thing to be studied and evaluated against a Western standard. Rather, cultural values should be appreciated and understood within their own context.

Finally, risk assessment presents several ethical challenges. A provider's personal beliefs and values can interfere with accurate assessment. Judgments can reflect personal biases, past experiences, or the amount of information available, more than the actual risk involved. Different providers can use varying techniques for obtaining and evaluating information, creating inconsistencies in the field (McCurdy, 1995). Providers must be careful when using clinical expertise so as not to make intuitive judgments based on factors other than recognition of actual risk. When completing evaluations, providers should be aware of the values of their profession, like respecting client autonomy, respecting human dignity, and encouraging self-determination (Badarau, 2015). The ethics of risk assessment are covered further in Chapter 9.

ASSESSING PARENT FACTORS

Parent risk and protective factors should be carefully assessed. Information about these variables can be obtained from clinical interviews, collateral interviews, self-report measures, standardized tests and instruments, observational assessments, and qualitative assessments. Sources of information can include parents, children, extended family, teachers, family friends, neighbors, other providers, etc. Risk and protective factors are detailed in Chapter 4. Providers should use various methods of assessment to obtain a thorough understanding of each family. Keep in mind when assessing parent behavior that parents can behave differently, communicate differently, and use different forms of discipline and parenting with different children. For this reason, it is important to observe and inquire about parent qualities associated with each child in the family. Table 5.1 outlines necessary information to obtain and questions to answer when assessing parent factors.

ASSESSING CHILD FACTORS

Unfortunately, some individual child factors can put children at greater risk for maltreatment. Variables that children have no control over like sex, age, and neurodevelopment are all linked to increased rates of maltreatment. Child factors can be assessed through clinical interviews, collateral interviews, self-report measures, standardized tests and instruments, observational assessments, and qualitative assessments. Children can be good sources of information themselves, but special care must be taken when interviewing children so as not to further traumatize them, and not to taint their reports. Children can be highly suggestible, and their testimonies are easily influenced by adults who ask leading questions. Considerations for interviewing children are detailed in Chapter 6.

Table 5.1 Assessing Parent Factors

Mental Health	Mental health disorders – particularly depression, schizophrenia, bipolar disorder Developmental delays Mental health characteristics – particularly anger, hyperreactivity, impulsiveness, paranoia, grandiosity, hallucinations, delusions Comorbid disorders What is the parent's stress level? What is causing this parent stress? Are these stressors likely short-term or long-term?
Personality	Personality disorders Level of empathy Locus of control Level of self-esteem Personality traits – hostility, impulsivity, domineering style, apathy, sociopathy Quality of interpersonal skills Level of emotional intelligence
Level of Functioning	Social competence Problem solving skills Cognitive flexibility Level of insight Intellectual functioning (can be formally measured through intelligence testing) Level of education How does the parent cope with stress? Does the parent have the internal and external resources needed to cope with stress?
Substance Use	Does the parent use substances? Does the parent's substance use indicate a substance use disorder? Does the parent's substance use impede ability to care for a child? Is substance use comorbid with a mental health condition or intimate partner violence?
Parent Attitudes	Level of parenting stress How does the parent interact with the child during play? Do they engage in stimulating activities? Does the parent respond appropriately to the child's bids for attention? Does the parent use appropriate vocal and facial responses with the child? Is the parent aware of child development stages and needs? Does the parent ascribe malintent to the child's behavior? Does the parent perceive the child as challenging?

Table 5.1 Cont.

	Does the parent have reasonable expectations of the child?
	Does the parent respond to the child in a consistent manner?
	What is the method of discipline? Is the parent flexible in their discipline?
	Does the parent provide reasonable instructions to the child?
	Does the parent praise the child?
	Does the parent criticize the child?
	Was the child wanted?
Family Structure and Stability	Parent age
	Are there one or two parents in the household?
	Is the family structure often changing?
	Who resides in the home? Are the residents consistent?
	Who is primarily responsible for the child?
	Who supervises the child?
	Are family roles flexible?
	Who is responsible for disciplining the child?
	What is the quality of the family's communication style? Is it cooperative or combative?
	Is treatment of the child consistent among parents?
	How often does the family move homes? When was the most recent move?
	Has a parent been absent for an extended period of time?
Parent History of Maltreatment	Does the parent have a history of child maltreatment?
	What kind(s) of child maltreatment did the parent experience?
	How was the parent nurtured as a child?
	How was the parent disciplined as a child?
	What is the parent's attachment style?
	Does the parent have a history of violence or intimate partner violence in their family-of-origin?
	What is the parent's view and level of insight into the way they were parented?
History of Violence	History of intimate partner violence
	History of family violence
	Current intimate partner violence
	Current family violence
	History of violence outside the family
	Criminal or incarceration history
Prior Child Welfare History	History of child welfare reports
	History of child removal
	History of termination of parental rights

Table 5.1 Cont.

Culture	Immigration status
	Acculturative stress
	Acculturative differences between parents and children
	Harmful cultural practices
	Are there any cultural norms that can obscure child
	    maltreatment or impede disclosure?
	Does the family experience discrimination?
	Did the family become fractured through immigration or
	    ethnic conflict?

Protective Factors	Self-esteem Self-efficacy Coping skills Social support Is the parent bonded to the child? Is the parent motivated to change? Does the parent seek help and utilize resources? Is the family's culture a source of support?

Additional sources of information include extended family, family friends, and neighbors. Teachers, school administrators, and daycare workers can be valuable sources for gathering information about children's behaviors and characteristics. Child risk factors are detailed in Chapter 4. While child protective factors can be assessed, they typically do not help prevent maltreatment. Rather, child protective factors can help children cope with the effects of maltreatment and be more resilient. For this reason, they are not included in this section. Table 5.2 outlines necessary information to obtain and questions to answer when assessing child factors.

ASSESSING ENVIRONMENTAL FACTORS

Environmental factors encompass the overarching challenges families might face. Socioeconomic status, neighborhood crime, and social isolation can all contribute to risk of maltreatment. These are detailed further in Chapter 4. This information can be gathered through

Table 5.2 Assessing Child Factors

Identifying Characteristics	Child age
	Can the child take care of some of their needs?
	Can the child protect themselves?
	Was the child born prematurely?
	Child gender
	Does the child identify as LGBT?
	Does the child have medical needs?
Mental Health Characteristics	Behavioral problems
	Mental health disorders
	Does the child have a difficult temperament?
	Does the child have emotional challenges?
	Intellectual disability
	Learning disorders
	Autism spectrum disorder
	Other neurodevelopmental disorders

self-report and knowledge about specific community characteristics in the neighborhood in which the family resides. Sources of information are typically parents, teachers and other community members, and public information and statistics about a particular community.

Table 5.3 outlines necessary information to obtain and questions to answer when assessing environmental factors.

ASSESSMENT INSTRUMENTS

An array of actuarial instruments is available for assessing various domains that contribute to risk. Standardized tests like the Weschler Adult Intelligence Scale (WAIS) can be used to determine parents' intellectual functioning. The Minnesota Multiphasic Personality Inventory-2 (MMPI-2) is commonly used to assess parent personality and traits. Self-report measures are useful for assessing other areas. The DSM-5 Level 1 Cross-Cutting Symptom Measure can detect any parent mental health symptoms and the Substance Abuse Subtle Screening Inventory (SASSI) can detect substance use problems. Child behavioral inventories can be administered to teachers and parents and maltreatment checklists can be

Table 5.3 Assessing Environmental Factors

Socioeconomic Status	Is the family financially stable? Can they pay their monthly expenses consistently? Does the family have the financial resources to cover an emergency? How long could the family survive if a parent were to lose their employment? Is the family's yearly income below the poverty line? Does the parent have stable and relatively secure employment? How much work stress does the parent experience? How safe are the parent's work environments? Does the parent receive paid sick leave and paid time off? Does the family have health insurance? Was a parent recently terminated from their employment?
Neighborhood Risk Factors	Is the average family income in this neighborhood below the poverty line? Is the family's housing stable or is there a risk of eviction or other removal from their home? What is the rate of violence in the neighborhood? What is the rate of crime in the neighborhood? Is there gang violence in the neighborhood? Is it safe for children to play outside? Is there clean running water? Is the home safe from physical hazards? Is the neighborhood (parks, playgrounds, sidewalks, etc.) safe from physical hazards like broken glass, drug paraphernalia, broken equipment, hazardous debris? Can the family access food, schools, medical care, and other basic needs?
Social Support	Who is in the parent's social support network? What is the parent's level of social support? What is the parent's *perceived* level of social support? Does the parent know how to access and utilize their social support networks? Does the parent know who to turn to for specific problems? Does the parent know how to form and maintain relationships? Is the parent willing to ask for help? Is the support network positive and encouraging? Does the parent have access to community support like afterschool programs?

used with children. Some instruments are specifically constructed to assess risk factors associated with maltreatment. The following are self-report and observational assessment tools for assessing maltreatment risk.

CHILD ABUSE POTENTIAL (CAP) INVENTORY

The Child Abuse Potential (CAP) Inventory (Milner, 1986) is 160-item actuarial parent self-report questionnaire designed to assess parental risk in cases where maltreatment is suspected. Seventy-seven of the items address child physical abuse. This instrument has six subscales: Distress, Rigidity, Unhappiness, Problems with Child and Self, Problems with Family, and Problems with Others. This instrument also includes an ego-strength scale and a loneliness scale as well as three validity scales: the lie scale, the random response scale, and the inconsistency scale to detect for respondents faking good and faking bad. The CAP Inventory can be completed in 10–20 minutes. Internal consistency ranges from .92 to .95 and can range from .85 to .96 with different ethnic and cultural groups.

BRIGID COLLINS RISK SCREENER (BCRS)

The Brigid Collins Risk Screener (BCRS) is a brief prenatal actuarial self-report questionnaire used in conjunction with medical records. This measure gives expectant parents a risk score based on groups of risk factors, single risk indicators, and protective factors. The BCRS is administered at the mother's first prenatal visit and assesses multiple factors including maternal health behaviors, maternal attitude about the pregnancy, mother's child-rearing history, socioeconomic status, and housing. The BCRS consists of four subscales: Environmental Stressors, Social Isolation, General Medical/Psychological Condition, and Nature of the Pregnancy. The BCRS was found to be consistent with similar instruments with strong reliability (Weberling et al., 2003).

CALDWELL HOME (HOME OBSERVATION FOR MEASUREMENT OF THE ENVIRONMENT) INVENTORY FOR INFANTS

The Caldwell HOME Inventory for Infants (Caldwell & Bradley, 1984) is an in-home interview and parent-child observation designed to assess the quality of an infant's home environment. This measure is administered by a provider observing parent-infant interactions within the home environment and observing characteristics of the home itself. The Caldwell HOME has six subscales: Maternal Emotional and Verbal Responsivity, Use of Punishment or Restriction, Organization of the Physical Environment, Availability of Developmentally Appropriate Play Items, Quality of Maternal-Child Interactions, and Opportunities for Variety in Child's Daily Life. This instrument is widely used to evaluate infant cognitive stimulation and emotional support. Internal consistency is .85 and interrater reliability is 94.2% (Boehm, 1985).

PARENTING STRESS INDEX, SHORT FORM (PSI/SF)

The Parenting Stress Index, Short Form (PSI/SF) (Abidin, 1990) is a 36-item paper and pencil self-report questionnaire that asks respondents to rate their level of agreement with parenting statements on a five-point scale. This measure is designed to be completed by parents or other caregivers. The PSI/SF consists of four subscales: Parent Stress, Parent-Child Difficult Interaction, Difficult Child, and Defensive Responding. The first three scales assess problematic parenting while the fourth scale identifies defensiveness in responses. The PSI/SF has a two-week test-retest reliability of r = .95 (Abidin, 1990).

INSTRUMENT FOR IDENTIFICATION OF PARENTS AT RISK FOR CHILD ABUSE AND NEGLECT (IPARAN)

The Instrument for Identification of Parents at Risk for Child Abuse and Neglect (IPARAN) (van der Put et al., 2017) is a 16-item self-report actuarial instrument for early detection of families at risk of child maltreatment. This instrument is based on the bioecological model (Belsky, 1980; Bronfenbrenner, 1979) and assesses families across three domains: parental personality and developmental history (ontogenic factors); child and family characteristics (microsystem); and social context (exosystem). This instrument is designed to be completed by parents and asks questions about parental attitudes, parenting stress, social support, parent's childhood history, substance use, attitudes toward corporal punishment, and violence or anger issues. The IPARAN was found to have strongest predictive validity when combined with clinical judgment (van der Put et al., 2017).

CHILD ABUSE RISK ASSESSMENT SCALE

The Child Abuse Risk Assessment Scale (CARAS) (Chan, 2012) is a 64-item actuarial self-report instrument for detection of risk of physical abuse. The CARAS contains 14 subscales: Anger Management, Violence Approval, Depressive Symptoms, Social Desirability, Stressful Conditions, Substance Abuse, Childhood Witnessed Parental IPV, In-law Conflict, Social Support, Self-Esteem, Sexual Abuse History, Criminal History, Preceding-Year IPV, and Preceding-Year Corporal Punishment. Subscales assess factors the research has found to be associated with child maltreatment. This measure is designed to be completed by parents. CARAS was found to have sensitivity = 82%, specificity = 78%, and overall accuracy = 78% (Chan, 2012).

CASE STUDY

The Stevens family was referred for a risk evaluation after receiving services from the local child welfare agency and the worker assigned to their cases indicated suspicion of child neglect and physical abuse. Mr Stevens is a 26-year-old white male and Mrs Stevens is a 23-year-old white female. Together, they have two children, a six-month-old female, Jasmine, and three-year-old male, Jameson. The child protective worker assigned to the Stevens' case noted Jasmine had a very soiled diaper during two home visits and Jameson had a bruise on his face. The child welfare agency determined some indicators of neglect but could not confirm any indicators of physical abuse. Both parents successfully completed a parenting course and Jameson was enrolled in subsidized daycare. Before withdrawing supervision, the child welfare agency requires an assessment for future risk.

Mr Stevens is the primary breadwinner for the family, working in a sheet metal factory. He reports working long hours, that his employer does not offer many benefits and that his job can be dangerous at times. Mrs Stevens stays home with the children and earns extra money by babysitting other children in the neighborhood. She can sometimes have up to six children in her home at once. Neither Mr nor Mrs Stevens graduated high school though Mr Stevens obtained his GED during his time in a juvenile detention center at age 17. Mrs Stevens has a history of maltreatment herself, having been removed from her childhood family home at age eight and subsequently being raised by her grandmother, after spending two years in the foster care system.

Both of the Stevens' children had normal pregnancies and deliveries. The mother reports that both children were 'a surprise' but that she and the father are happy to have them. She reports experiencing post-partum depression after having the first child though she did not seek treatment. Because of her childhood experiences, Mrs Stevens' parents are not a source of support for the family. Her grandmother sometimes watches the children, though Mrs Stevens reports she is aging and less able to care for children. Mrs Stevens identifies a few friends she considers sources of support. Mr Stevens' mother sometimes cares for the children, but the parents report she can be inconsistent and is sometime difficult to contact. The family resides in a two-bedroom apartment in a lower SES neighborhood.

CASE STUDY DISCUSSION PROMPTS

1. Upon initial evaluation, list the risk and protective factors that are immediately apparent.
2. List the assessment strategies and instruments you would use to evaluate the Stevens family.
3. List the sources of information you would utilize in evaluating the Stevens family.

SUMMARY

This chapter discussed how to assess risk and protective factors using the bioecological model. Census-based and actuarial forms of assessment were outlined and obstacles to assessment were explored. Assessment across parent, child, and environmental domains was detailed, including questions to answer in each respective area and useful assessment instruments.

REFERENCES

Abidin, R. (1990). *Parenting stress index short form*. Pediatric Psychology Press.

Badarau, O. L. (2015). Ethical dilemmas in the risk assessment of recurrent child maltreatment in the family. *Revista de Asistenja Sociala, 14,* 39–46.

Belsky, J. (1980). Child maltreatment: An ecological integration. *American Psychologist, 35*(4), 320–335. https://doi.org/10.1037/0003-066x.35.4.320

Boehm, A. (1985). Review of home observation for measurement of the environment. In J. Mitchell (Ed.), *The ninth mental measurements yearbook*. University of Nebraska Press.

Bronfenbrenner, U. (1979). *The ecology of human development: Experiments by nature and design*. Harvard University Press.

Caldwell, B., & Bradley, R. (1984). *Home observation for measurement of the environment*. University of Arkansas at Little Rock Press.

Chan, K. L. (2012). Evaluating the risk of child abuse: The Child Abuse Risk Assessment Scale (CARAS). *Journal of Interpersonal Violence, 27*(5), 951–973.

Cicchetti, D., & Valentino, K. (2006). An ecological-transactional perspective on child maltreatment: Failure of the average expectable environment and its influence on child development. In D. Cicchetti & D. J. Cohen (Eds.), *Developmental psychopathology: Risk, disorder, and adaptation*. Wiley. https://doi.org/10.1002/9780470939406.ch4

Levenson, J. S., & Morin, J. W. (2006). Risk assessment in child sexual abuse cases. *Child Welfare, 85*(1), 59–82.

McCurdy, K. (1995). Risk assessment in child abuse prevention programs. *Social Work Research, 19*(2), 77–87. https://doi.org/10.1093/swr/19.2.77

Milner, J. S. (1986). *The child abuse potential inventory: Manual* (2nd edn). Psytec.

Righthand, S., Kerr, B. B., & Drach, K. (2003). *Child maltreatment risk assessments: An evaluation guide*. Taylor & Francis.

Sperry, L. (2019). Choosing effective couple and family assessment methods. In L. Sperry (Ed). *Couple and family assessment: Contemporary and cutting-edge strategies* (3rd edn). Routledge.

Stroud, J., & Warren-Adamson, C. (2013). Multi-agency child protection: Can risk assessment frameworks be helpful? *Social Work and Social Sciences Review, 16*(3), 37–49. https://doi.org/10.1921/3703160304

van der Put, C. E., Bouwmeester-Landweer, M. B., Landsmeer-Beker, E. A., Wit, J. M., Dekker, F. W., Kousemaker, N. J., & Baartman, H. E. (2017). Screening for potential child maltreatment in parents of a newborn baby: The predictive validity of an instrument for early identification of parents at risk for child abuse and neglect (IPARAN). *Child Abuse & Neglect, 70*, 160–168. https://doi.org/10.1016/j.chiabu.2017.05.016

Weberling, L. C., Forgays, D. K., Crain-Thoreson, C., & Hyman, I. (2003). Prenatal child abuse risk assessment: A preliminary validation study. *Child Welfare, 82*(3), 319–334.

CHAPTER SIX

Assessing Children for Maltreatment

Assessing risk for future maltreatment requires assessing if maltreatment has already occurred. Child maltreatment assessment can also be prompted by a report, admission, or suspicion of abuse or neglect. Evaluating maltreatment can be much like evaluating risk. As violence is difficult to assess and predict, providers must rely on identifying factors that indicate harm. Similarly, evidence for maltreatment might not always be clear, leaving providers to analyze risk factors, parent factors, and environmental factors to estimate if maltreatment has occurred. Best practices in assessment include gathering information according to the bioecological approach, using multiple assessment strategies, and paying attention to influencing factors like observation effects, leading questions, and interview environment.

SYMPTOMS VS INCIDENTS

As introduced in Chapter 1, one cannot evaluate an event, in itself, to determine risk for future violence or harm. Providers can only complete an evaluation of physical and psychological symptoms arising from an event (Binensztok & Vastardis, 2019). For example, one cannot view a past incident of physical punishment and determine if it equates to physical abuse. One can only observe resulting bruises or marks, the child's behavior, the parent's behavior and history of violence, and the interactions between parent and child to make the most well-informed determination that abuse has or has not occurred. Unfortunately, some children might not show symptoms right away. Additionally, psychological, emotional, and behavioral symptoms are evaluated according to the Diagnostic and Statistical Manual-5 (DSM-5), yet there is no diagnosis for child maltreatment. This presents a confounding factor to evaluation as providers must, instead, assess the presence of psychological symptoms that correlate with maltreatment. The symptoms resulting from child abuse and neglect also rarely align with the criteria of any single psychological disorder, making it more difficult to determine if maltreatment is present. As discussed in Chapter 1 and

Chapter 3, though they have endured trauma, children who experienced maltreatment often do not meet criteria for posttraumatic stress disorder because this diagnosis was created to encompass the symptoms associated with Type I, or single-event, traumas while abused children experience Type II, or complex trauma. A more appropriate diagnosis for these children would be developmental trauma disorder (Hudspeth, 2015), but because this disorder does not exist in the DSM, abused children are often diagnosed with comorbid disorders or receive no diagnosis at all. Despite these challenges, providers must keep in mind the scope of their assessment and remember that though a retrospective account of incidents can be obtained, symptom evaluation is the most accurate way of determining harm.

FORMS OF ASSESSMENT

Different forms of assessment are useful in evaluating if child maltreatment has occurred. Sperry (2019) outlines four types of assessment – qualitative, standardized, observational, and self-report. Qualitative assessment uses unstructured interviewing and creative approaches to family storytelling to assess family characteristics and dynamics. Standardized assessment involves administering structured, normed tests and instruments to evaluate individual characteristics. Observational assessment can consist of observation of children, parent-child interactions, rearing practices, and family environment. Self-report assessments include clinical interviews and self-report measures that elicit information from children, parents, and related parties (Sperry, 2019). These forms of assessment are detailed further in Chapter 5. In child maltreatment assessment, standardized, observational, and self-report methods are most commonly used though qualitative methods may be useful as well. A thorough evaluation would include family observations, interviews with parents and children (if possible), and use of structured instruments.

SOURCES OF INFORMATION

A ssessments should use information gathered from various sources. Evaluators can gather information from past records, children, parents, and collateral sources. Collateral sources include people who are in close proximity to the child or family.

RECORDS

Children's school, daycare, medical, and dental records can be useful for identifying risk factors, warning signs, and patterns. For example, if a child missed important medical appointments, is not up-to-date on vaccinations, or has not had a regular medical or dental checkup as recommended, one might suspect some form of neglect. Frequent absences and late arrivals at school can signal some sort of family disarray. Receiving subsidized lunch or aftercare might indicate financial problems but also point to the positive use of community services. Children's behavioral reports from schools and daycares can indicate symptoms associated with maltreatment. For example, frequent fighting or sexualized behaviors are red flags for physical or sexual abuse, respectively. Some minors might have juvenile detention records that can also prove useful. Records of past maltreatment reports, investigations, and cases can reveal patterns that might point to current abuse or neglect. Parent police reports can help determine if there are documented incidents of violence that indicate or coincided with suspected abuse.

CHILDREN AND PARENTS

Verbal children can report incidents and detail what occurs in the home. While children can provide valuable information, providers should take certain precautions when interviewing children, so as not to influence their reports. Providers should also keep in mind that different children in the home can have different experiences with parents. Therefore, reports should be acquired from all verbal children in the home, including biological children, step-children, foster or adopted children, etc.

Parents can give insight into their parenting and discipline practices as well as their general attitude toward parenting. They can reveal abuse incidents and detail the family's challenges and resources. They can provide information about children's behavior, developmental course, and functioning. Considerations for assessing children and parents are discussed further in the sections below.

COLLATERAL SOURCES

Collateral sources of information include anyone who observes or interacts with the child or family. Teachers, school administrators, and daycare workers can provide useful information about children's behavior and whether they have ever observed any indicators of possible maltreatment like bruises, dirty clothing, or being sent to school or daycare without food or proper supplies. These professionals can also complete surveys and instruments evaluating children's behavior. Teachers can comment on parental involvement, consistency, and interpersonal skills. Extended relatives, neighbors, and family friends might not interact with children as often as teachers, but can still attest to indicators of maltreatment. They can report if they have witnessed children playing or staying home unattended, if children have been unkempt or hungry, if there is family conflict, and other insights into family dynamics.

THE BIOECOLOGICAL APPROACH TO INFORMATION GATHERING

Child maltreatment can be understood as the interaction of short-term and long-term events occurring on multiple levels of the child's ecology (Belsky, 1980). Based on Bronfenbrenner's (1979) theory of human development, and Belsky's (1980) adaptation of the bioecological model to child maltreatment, assessment encompasses microsystem, mesosystem, exosystem, macrosystem, and ontogenic factors. Microsystem level factors include the child's caregivers, peers, schools, and other daily interactions. Mesosystem level factors represent connections between multiple levels, i.e. how parents interact with school officials and other important figures in the child's life. Exosystem level factors represent children's neighborhoods, local governments, and other larger influences. Macrosystem level factors represent greater social norms and values. Ontogenic factors are individual to children and caregivers. It is important for evaluators to consider all information in context. Symptoms and indicators, themselves, are often not sufficient to conclude maltreatment has or has not occurred. Multiple indicators from different bioecological levels, and the interactions between them, should be considered together when assessing for maltreatment. More details on the bioecological model can be found in Chapter 5.

EVALUATING PARENTS

When assessing parents, providers should obtain information about parental attitudes, discipline styles, child rearing practices, and knowledge about child development. Aside from the admission of child maltreatment, much of this information is similar to what would be collected for a risk assessment. As previously stated, because maltreatment incidents are difficult to determine, providers rely on assessing indicators related to maltreatment. Clinical interviews, parent-child observations, and structured instruments can be used to evaluate parents. Observations can include direct observation of parent-child behavior during ordinary tasks like meals, bathing, and playing or through role-plays between parents and the provider (Gershater-Molko et al., 2003).

Information about parental attitudes addresses parenting stress, attachment, as well as the parent's level of reactivity toward the child.

Table 6.1 Evaluating Parents

Forms of Assessment	Clinical interview Self-report instruments Observation
Sources of Information	Parents Children Collateral sources Police records Child maltreatment records
Instruments	The Parent Behavior Checklist The Child Well-Being Scale The Parent-Child Conflict Tactics Scale The Dyadic Parent-Child Interaction Coding System The Behavioral Coding System The Home Simulation Assessment The Ontario Child Neglect Index Scale for Communicating the Likelihood of Sexual Abuse

Parent attitudes and views can indicate which parents are more likely to abuse or neglect their children. Parents who are more likely to have mistreated their children tend to view their children as more challenging and view their behavior as combative (Curenton et al., 2009; Righthand et al., 2003; Stith et al., 2009). Parents who strongly endorse corporal punishment might lack other disciplinary skills or be more likely to cross the line from corporal punishment to physical abuse. Parents who are not aware of child development and typical child needs and behaviors can be more likely to attribute negative intention to their children's behavior, increasing their likelihood of responding in an abusive manner (Stith et al., 2009). Table 6.1 outlines strategy for evaluating parents.

PARENT INSTRUMENTS

Self-report instruments and observational checklists are valuable for obtaining information about parents. Self-report instruments can assess parents' behavior, discipline style, and likelihood of abusing or neglecting children. The Parent Behavior Checklist (Fox, 1994) is a self-report questionnaire that assesses parenting skills across three subscales – discipline, nurturing, and expectations of child behavior. The Child Well-Being Scale (Magura & Moses, 2004) contains 43 subscales across parent and child domains. Subscales address the following areas of functioning – parenting role performance, familial capacities, child role performance, and child capacities. The Parent-Child Conflict Tactics Scale (Straus et al., 1998) is a 22-item self-report measure of parent-child conflict management and discipline. This instrument helps determine if physical abuse is present by assessing the following categories: nonviolent discipline, psychological aggression, and physical assault. Nonviolent discipline refers to common discipline strategies that do not involve corporal punishment. Psychological aggression refers to verbal or physical acts intended to trigger fear or emotional distress in a child. Physical assault refers to a range of physical punishments.

Observational instruments include The Dyadic Parent-Child Interaction Coding System (Robinson & Eyberg, 1981) and the Behavioral Coding System (Forehand & McMahon, 1981). The Dyadic Parent-Child Interaction Coding System assesses child behaviors like crying, yelling, compliance, opposition, and destructive behavior, as well as parent behaviors like use of instructions, critical statements, praise statements, and commands. The Behavioral Coding System assesses parental use of attention, questions, commands, warnings, consequences, and rewards. Observations of direct parent-child interactions are preferable to assess relationship dynamics, but this might not always be feasible. In this case, an adult can role-play scenarios with a parent (Gershater-Molko et al., 2003). The Home Simulation Assessment (HAS) (MacMillan et al., 1991) is an observational checklist that gauges how parents manage difficult child behaviors. The HAS engages parents in ten role-play scenarios, during which child behavior management skills are observed.

Instruments completed by professionals include The Ontario Child Neglect Index (Trocme, 1996) and the Scale for Communicating the Likelihood of Sexual Abuse (Melville & Lindberg, 2020). The Ontario Child Neglect Index is a brief instrument with six neglect subscales including supervision, nutrition, clothing and hygiene, physical health care, mental health care, and development/educational care. The Scale for Communicating the Likelihood of Sexual Abuse is a six-point scale designed to be completed by child abuse pediatricians. Medical providers rate the likelihood of sexual abuse from 'no sexual abuse concerns,' to 'clearly indicates sexual abuse' (Melville & Lindberg, 2020).

EVALUATING CHILDREN

Children who have been abused and neglected often display emotional and behavioral problems (Binensztok & Vastardis, 2019). Children can exhibit symptoms of depression and anxiety. They can also show problems with emotional regulation, impulse control, aggression, and other behavioral problems. One of the hallmark signs of sexual abuse in children is sexualized behavior (Binensztok & Vastardis, 2019). Children might touch their genitals at inappropriate times or in inappropriate ways, or perform sexual acts with other children. Of course, no single child behavior can guarantee that maltreatment has occurred. Emotional and behavioral symptoms can exist in the absence of abuse and, like other variables, should be evaluated within the context of the child's greater ecology. Child observations, clinical interviews with verbal children, and use of standardized instruments are required for child assessment. Observations and interviews with children can also assess qualitative factors by using creative methods like play therapy, sandtray, puppets, etc. Instruments can be administered to children, depending on reading level, to parents, or to other adults who regularly interact with the child, like teachers. Providers can use records of behavioral infractions at school, juvenile detention records, medical records, and psychiatric records to gather more information about the child's behavior. Medical records can also detail if there have been any physical indicators of abuse like bruises or lacerations in the case of physical abuse, malnourishment in the case of neglect, and injury to the genitals or sexually transmitted infections in the case of sexual abuse. Table 6.2 outlines strategy for evaluating children.

Table 6.2 Evaluating Children

Forms of Assessment	Clinical interview Self-report instruments Observation Qualitative methods
Sources of Information	Parents Children Collateral sources School records Daycare records Medical records Psychiatric records Behavioral records
Instruments	The Adverse Childhood Experience Scale Eyberg Child Behavior Inventory Child Behavior Checklist

CHILD INSTRUMENTS

Few instruments assess the presence of child maltreatment. Rather, instruments used to evaluate maltreatment more often assess the emotional and behavioral symptoms associated with maltreatment. One instrument that does assess if maltreatment has occurred is the Adverse Childhood Experience (ACE) scale (Felitti et al., 1998). The ACE scale is a ten-question yes/no response instrument that inquires if a child experienced physical abuse, sexual abuse, psychological abuse, witnessed domestic violence or substance use, and other forms of maltreatment. Children old enough to understand the language in this scale can self-report incidents of abuse.

One measure of child behavior associated with maltreatment is the Eyberg Child Behavior Inventory (Eyberg & Ross, 1978). This widely used instrument uses 36 items to assess child behavior problems on a seven-point scale of intensity in children aged two to 16. Another instrument, the Child Behavior Checklist (Achenbach & Edelbrook, 1983) assesses child behavioral problems across the following domains – Schizoid/ Anxious, Depressed, Uncommunicative, Obsessive-Compulsive, Somatic Complaints, Social Withdrawal, Ineffective, Aggressive, and Delinquent.

This 118-item instrument can be used for children aged two to 16. Child behavior instruments can be administered to parents, teachers, and other adults prominent in the child's daily life. Because abusive parents are more likely to rate their children's behavior as difficult or problematic, comparing scores between parents and other adults on the same instruments can also give providers information on parent attitudes.

INTERVIEWING CHILDREN

Special considerations are warranted when interviewing children. Interviews can be a frightening experience for children. Children can be intimidated by adults asking them questions, some of which are sensitive in nature (Aldridge & Wood, 1998). They might have been instructed not to speak to strangers or might worry they are being interviewed because they are in trouble or did something wrong. Children can also experience further trauma when recounting incidents of abuse. Interviews should be conducted in a gentle and supportive manner to minimize the stress children can experience when being interviewed. Providers must also conduct interviews using language and concepts that are developmentally appropriate for children.

In response to a landscape fraught with error in child interviewing, the Memorandum of Good Practice (1992) was developed to provide a set of guidelines for interviewing children. The memorandum suggests interviewing in phases, and not exceeding one hour of interview time in a sitting. Interview phases consist of a rapport building phase, a free narrative phase, a questioning phase, and a closure phase. In the rapport building phase, the provider asks the child about hobbies, interests, and other general questions. In the free narrative phase, the child is allowed to recount events at their own pace. In the questioning phase, the provider asks the child more pointed questions about the events, and in the closure phase, the child is allowed to ask questions and the interview is summarized and brought to a close (Aldridge & Wood, 1998; Sternberg et al., 2001).

The provider should consider the location of the interview, whether or not an adult will accompany the child, and other considerations for the child's comfort. The provider should clearly explain the purpose of the interview and assure the child that they have done nothing wrong. If the interview is being recorded, this should be explained to the child as well. The provider should explain that the child might not know the answers to some questions and that is an acceptable response. The provider can use toys and games to facilitate rapport with the child and should be careful not to rush into the questioning phase too quickly. The provider should use words the child understands and explain important words that the child is either unfamiliar with or that mean something different to the child than the provider (Aldridge & Wood, 1998).

Everyone is vulnerable to false memories and leading questions, but children are particularly at risk for these complications. Children might not recall certain events or might not yet possess the schemas and language needed to recall the details of events (Fivush, 2002). In their landmark study, Loftus and Pickrell (1995) found that up to 25% of adults questioned about childhood events were subject to having false memories implanted. Children are significantly more vulnerable to developing false memories. One study showed that 58% of participating children endorsed a false memory after being asked to imagine both real and false events and then being consistently questioned about those events (Ceci et al., 1994).

One of the reasons children are more susceptible to false memories is their high level of suggestibility (Lamb et al., 2008). Leading questions can increase the likelihood that a child will endorse a false narrative. Questions found to be most likely to elicit a false response were those that presumed facts or incidents that were not previously mentioned by the child, and those that included very specific details (Hughes-Scholes & Powell, 2008). Best practice interview guidelines encourage children to state things in their own words rather than the provider constructing a scene of the event for the child (Powell et al., 2005). There is an abundance of research on the theory and practice of forensic interviewing of children that is too great for the scope of this book but should be explored before conducting maltreatment interviews.

EVALUATING ENVIRONMENT

Similar to assessment of parent factors, evaluating environment in child maltreatment resembles the risk assessment process. Providers should incorporate information about the child's home environment, neighborhood, and parent functioning outside the home, including parents' level of social support. This information can be acquired through observation and self-report measures. Keep in mind that while some environmental factors might strongly point to maltreatment, others might be present in the absence of maltreatment. For example, a family whose home is unsanitary or unsafe might be more likely to be neglecting their children but a family who lacks social support, a crucial resource, might not be maltreating their children. Table 6.3 outlines strategy for evaluating environment.

Table 6.3 Evaluating Environment

Forms of Assessment	Clinical interview Observation instruments
Sources of Information	Parents Children Collateral sources Public records
Instruments	The Well-Child Care Visit, Evaluation, Community Resources, Advocacy, Referral, Education (WE-CARE) screen The Home Accident Prevention Inventory Checklist for Living Environments to Assess Neglect (CLEAN) The Eco Map The Perceived Social Support Questionnaire

ENVIRONMENT INSTRUMENTS

Some instruments and checklists exist to help providers evaluate children's environments. These instruments focus on parental resources and the general home environment. One such instrument is the Well-Child Care Visit, Evaluation, Community Resources, Advocacy, Referral, Education (WE-CARE) screen (Garg et al., 2007). The WE-CARE screen is a ten-item survey that assesses parent need for employment, education, childcare, and housing. This instrument also screens for tobacco use, substance use, domestic violence, food insecurity, and depression.

The Home Accident Prevention Inventory (HAPI) (Tertinger et al., 1984) assesses physical hazards present in the home, including hazards that can cause death. This checklist divides hazards into the following categories: suffocation by ingestible objects, suffocation by mechanical objects, fire and electrical hazards, firearms, hazardous sharp objects, and poisonous solids and liquids. Falling and drowning hazards are also noted as well as the accessibility of hazards to children. The Checklist for Living Environments to Assess Neglect (CLEAN) (Watson-Perczel et al., 1988) evaluates the level of clutter and cleanliness in a home. The CLEAN addresses the following dimensions: presence of objects not belonging in a certain area, presence of clothes and linen not belonging in a certain area, and presence of organic or nonorganic decaying matter. The Eco Map (Hartman, 1978) assesses the family's ecology and level of social support using a visual map. The Perceived Social Support Questionnaire (Procidano & Heller, 1983) assesses social support as well as if the parent feels they are able to access this support.

OBSTACLES TO ASSESSMENT

Unfortunately, there are many obstacles to accurate assessment of child maltreatment. As previously discussed, though they can obtain retrospective accounts of events, providers struggle to accurately assess these events as to whether or not they are abusive. Thus, they must assess symptoms and risk factors for maltreatment. This presents a challenge because of misdiagnosis and comorbidity. Different forms of abuse and neglect often co-occur and it can be difficult to trace symptoms to a specific type of maltreatment (Stockhammer et al., 2001). Psychological abuse can be particularly difficult to assess because it leaves no physical indicators and is often less detectable in the absence of overt acts like intimate partner violence. Psychological abuse can also be overshadowed by co-occurring forms of abuse and neglect (Binensztok & Vastardis, 2019). Children who are neglected typically experience multiple forms of neglect. Neglect is also usually chronic but singular seemingly neglectful acts might not actually qualify as neglect. These factors make neglect difficult to assess and attribute to singular events (Stowman & Donohue, 2005). Emotional and behavioral symptoms related to abuse can also masquerade as other psychological disorders. Emotional dysregulation, self-harm, hypersexuality, suicidality, aggression, and social problems resulting from maltreatment can be mistaken for diagnoses like depression, anxiety, bipolar disorder, and oppositional defiant disorder (Binensztok & Vastardis, 2019).

Information sources can also pose challenges to assessment. Parents serve as the most common sources in child maltreatment cases, yet they are known to be unreliable informants (Binensztok & Vastardis, 2019; Stockhammer et al., 2001). Children can be valuable sources of information, but they can be threatened into denying or concealing abusive events. Children can also recant information or provide false information when subjected to leading testimony (Aldridge & Wood, 1998; Lamb et al., 2008). Using too few sources of information limits the accuracy of assessment (Enosh et al., 2019). Speaking to multiple sources and acquiring records can help with accuracy but records can be sparse or fail to provide relevant details (Binensztok & Vastardis, 2019). Culture can also affect how people respond to interviewing and language can interfere with both interviewing and use of instruments. Cultural differences can interfere with rapport building between clients and providers and people of varying cultures can view acts differently in terms of whether or not they are abusive.

Instruments can have limitations as well. Not all instruments are translated to different languages and can be culturally bound. Many maltreatment sequelae, like neuropsychological effects and long-term emotional problems, are not measured by instruments. Child neglect instruments often do not address severity and duration of neglect and can focus too narrowly on specific age ranges (Stowman & Donohue, 2005). Validity of self-report responses is difficult to ascertain as responders can be faking good or faking bad, resulting in false negatives and false positives. Known as social desirability bias, parents might want to paint themselves in a more favorable light in order to make a better impression or avoid legal repercussions. Social desirability bias can affect responses to personality inventories, attitudes inventories, and behavioral self-report measures (Stowman & Donohue, 2005). Parents are also more adept at reporting children's externalizing symptoms than internalizing symptoms (Stover & Berkowitz, 2005) and children can struggle to identify their own symptoms to report them in an interview or instrument (Binensztok & Vastardis, 2019).

Observational assessments can prove challenging because of the observer effect. Also known as the Hawthorne effect, observer effect refers to people's tendency to behave differently when they know they are being observed, even when they do not know which of their behaviors are being observed (McCambridge et al., 2014). Parents and children can behave differently than normal while under observation (Stowman & Donohue, 2005). Parent presence during child observation can also affect child behavior and presentation. One study found that children's task performance in neuropsychological testing was affected by parental presence during the testing (Yantz & McCaffrey, 2009). As in the case of risk assessment, obstacles to obtaining accurate information complicate child maltreatment assessment. Providers should take measures to minimize these challenges, understanding that some cases will remain difficult to discern.

CASE STUDY

Mason, a nine-year-old white male child, was placed in a foster care setting by the local child welfare agency after a medical doctor made a report to the child abuse reporting hotline. During a routine school-entrance physical, the medical doctor found evidence of an untreated injury to the child's wrist. It appeared the child had a sprained wrist as there was some swelling and a bruise later in the healing stage. An x-ray revealed a hairline fracture in Mason's right wrist, which appeared to have been present for about two to three weeks. When asked what happened, Mason's mother interjected and stated Mason had fallen off his bike about a week ago. When asked why she did not take the child to the hospital or urgent care, she stated, 'We didn't think it was that serious.' The doctor reported to the hotline operator that he was unsure of how the injury occurred but that he was concerned about medical neglect, at the very least considering the child had what appeared to have been a significant bruise at one point.

Upon entering the home, the caseworker noticed a lot of refuse in bags around the kitchen and living room. Though there were two bathrooms in the home, the toilet and faucet only worked in one. Some of the bricks were loose on the stairway to the home, and various hazardous materials were spotted outside, including cans of solvent and pieces of wood with nails protruding from them. Mason appeared unkempt and had holes in his shirt and shorts. The doctor had also noted an unkempt appearance. The caseworker removed the child and the dependency court judge ordered supervised visits between Mason and his parents. The judge ordered an evaluation of child maltreatment to help workers determine if maltreatment had occurred and what kind of maltreatment had occurred, if any, so they could decide how to proceed with this case.

CASE STUDY DISCUSSION PROMPTS

1. List the suspected forms of maltreatment present and describe the related indicators.
2. Describe which domains will need to be assessed and why.
3. Describe an assessment strategy. Which forms of assessment and instruments will be useful?

SUMMARY

Child maltreatment is similar to risk assessment in that it involves assessing risk factors across three domains – parent, child, and environment. Child maltreatment assessment, however, also evaluates other indicators of current or past maltreatment like children's symptoms. This chapter outlined forms of assessment and how to obtain information according to the bioecological model. Standardized instruments were described and obstacles to assessment were presented.

REFERENCES

Achenbach, T., & Edelbrook, C. S. (1983). *Manual for the child: Behavior checklist and revised child behavior profile.* University of Vermont.

Aldridge, M., & Wood, J. (1998). *Interviewing children: A guide for child care and forensic practitioners.* Wiley.

Belsky, J. (1980). Child maltreatment: An ecological integration. *American Psychologist, 35*(4), 320–335. https://doi.org/10.1037/0003-066x.35.4.320

Binensztok, V., & Vastardis, T. E. (2019). Child abuse assessment strategy and inventories. In L. Sperry (Ed.), *Couple and Family Assessment: Contemporary and Cutting-Edge Strategies* (3rd edn). Routledge.

Bronfenbrenner, U. (1979). *The ecology of human development: Experiments by nature and design.* Harvard University Press.

Ceci, S. J., Huffman, M., Smith, E., & Loftus, E. F. (1994). Repeatedly thinking about a non-event: Source misattributions among preschoolers. *Consciousness and Cognition, 3*(3–4), 388–407. https://doi.org/10.1006/ccog.1994.1022

Curenton, S. M., McWey, L. M., & Bolen, M. G. (2009). Distinguishing maltreating versus nonmaltreating at-risk families: Implications for foster care and early childhood education interventions. *Families in Society: The Journal of Contemporary Social Services, 90*(2), 176–182. https://doi.org/10.1606/1044-3894.3871

Enosh, G., Nouman, H., & Schneck, C. (2019). Child's religiosity, ethnic origin, and gender: A randomized experimental examination of risk assessment and placement decisions in cases of ambiguous risk to children from low SES families. *Research on Social Work Practice, 29*(7), 766–774. https://doi.org/10.1177/1049731518810795

Eyberg, S. M., & Ross, A. W. (1978). Assessment of child behavior problems: The validation of a new inventory. *Journal of Clinical Child Psychology, 7*(2), 113–116. https://doi.org/10.1080/15374417809532835

Felitti, V. J., Anda, R. F., Nordenberg, D., Williamson, D. F., Spitz, A. M., Edwards, V., Koss, M. P., & Marks, J. S. (1998). Relationship of childhood abuse and household dysfunction to many of the leading causes of death in adults. *American Journal of Preventive Medicine, 14*(4), 245–258. https://doi.org/10.1016/s0749-3797(98)00017-8

Fivush, R. (2002). The development of autobiographical memory. In H. L. Westcott, G. M. Davies, & R. Bull (Eds.), *Children's testimony: A handbook of psychological research and forensic practice*. Wiley.

Forehand, R., & McMahon, R. (1981). *Helping the noncompliant: A clinician's guide to parent training*. Guilford.

Fox, R. (1994). *Parent behavior checklist*. Clinical Psychology Pub. Co.

Garg, A., Butz, A. M., Dworkin, P. H., Lewis, R. A., Thompson, R. E., & Serwint, J. R. (2007). Improving the management of family psychosocial problems at low-income children's well-child care visits: The We Care project. *Pediatrics, 120*(3), 547–558. https://doi.org/10.1542/peds.2007-0398

Gershater-Molko, R. M., Lutzker, J. R., & Sherman, J. A. (2003). Assessing child neglect. *Aggression and Violent Behavior, 8*, 563–585.

Hartman, A. (1978). Diagrammatic assessments of family relationships. *Social Casework, 59*, 465–476.

Hudspeth, E. (2015). Children with special needs and circumstances: Conceptualization through a complex trauma lens. *The Professional Counselor*, 5(2), 195–199. https://doi.org/10.15241/efh.5.2.195

Hughes-Scholes, C. H., & Powell, M. B. (2008). An examination of the types of leading questions used by investigative interviewers of children. *Policing: An International Journal of Police Strategies & Management*, 31(2), 210–225. https://doi.org/10.1108/13639510810878695

Lamb, M. E., Orbach, Y., Sternberg, K. J., Esplin, P. W., & Hershkowitz, I. (2008). The effects of forensic interview practices on the quality of information provided by alleged victims of child abuse. In H. L. Westcott, G. M. Davies, R. H. C. Bull (Eds.), *Children's testimony*. John Wiley & Sons Ltd. https://doi.org/10.1002/9780470713679.ch9

Loftus, E. F., & Pickrell, J. E. (1995). The formation of false memories. *Psychiatric Annals*, 25(12), 720–725. https://doi.org/10.3928/0048-5713-19951201-07

MacMillan, V. M., Olson, R. L., & Hansen, D. J. (1991). Low and high deviance analogue assessment of parent-training with physically abusive parents. *Journal of Family Violence*, 6(3), 279–301. https://doi.org/10.1007/bf00980534

Magura, S., & Moses, B. S. (2004). *Outcome measures for child welfare services: Theory and applications*. Child Welfare League of Amer.

McCambridge, J., Witton, J., & Elbourne, D. R. (2014). Systematic review of the Hawthorne effect: New concepts are needed to study research participation effects. *Journal of Clinical Epidemiology*, 67(3), 267–277. https://doi.org/10.1016/j.jclinepi.2013.08.015

Melville, J. D., & Lindberg, D. M. (2020). A novel scale to communicate perceived likelihood of child sexual abuse. *Academic Pediatrics*, 20(4), 460–467. https://doi.org/10.1016/j.acap.2019.12.010

Powell, M. B., Fisher, R. P., & Wright, R. (2005). Investigative interviewing. In N. Brewer & K. Williams (Eds.), *Psychology and law: An empirical perspective*. Guilford.

Procidano, M. E., & Heller, K. (1983). Measures of perceived social support from friends and from family: Three validation studies. *American Journal of Community Psychology*, 11(1), 1–24. https://doi.org/10.1007/bf00898416

Righthand, S., Kerr, B. B., & Drach, K. (2003). *Child maltreatment risk assessments: An evaluation guide*. Taylor & Francis.

Robinson, E. A., & Eyberg, S. M. (1981). The dyadic parent–child interaction coding system: Standardization and validation. *Journal of Consulting and Clinical Psychology, 49*(2), 245–250. https://doi.org/10.1037/0022-006x.49.2.245

Sperry, L. (2019). Choosing effective couple and family assessment methods. In L. Sperry (Ed). *Couple and family assessment: Contemporary and cutting-edge strategies* (3rd edn). Routledge.

Sternberg, K. J., Lamb, M. E., Davies, G. M., & Westcott, H. L. (2001). The memorandum of good practice: Theory versus application. *Child Abuse & Neglect, 25*(5), 669–681. https://doi.org/10.1016/s0145-2134(01)00232-0

Stith, S. M., Liu, T., Davies, L., Boykin, E. L., Alder, M. C., Harris, J. M., Som, A., McPherson, M., & Dees, J. (2009). Risk factors in child maltreatment: A meta-analytic review of the literature. *Aggression and Violent Behavior, 14*(1), 13–29. https://doi.org/10.1016/j.avb.2006.03.006

Stockhammer, T. F., Salzinger, S., Feldman, R. S., & Mojica, E. (2001). Assessment of the effect of physical child abuse within an ecological framework: Measurement issues. *Journal of Community Psychology, 29*(3), 319–344.

Stover, C., & Berkowitz, S. (2005). Assessing violence exposure and trauma symptoms in young children: A critical review of measures. *Journal of Traumatic Stress, 18*(6), 707–717. https://doi.org/10.1002/jts.20079

Stowman, S. A., & Donohue, B. (2005). Assessing child neglect: A review of standardized measures. *Aggression and Violent Behavior, 10*(4), 491–512. https://doi.org/10.1016/j.avb.2004.08.001

Straus, M. A., Hamby, S. L., Finkelhor, D., Moore, D. W., & Runyan, D. (1998). Identification of child maltreatment with the parent-child conflict tactics scales: Development and psychometric data for a national sample of American parents. *Child Abuse & Neglect, 22*(4), 249–270. https://doi.org/10.1016/s0145-2134(97)00174-9

Tertinger, D. A., Greene, B. F., & Lutzker, J. R. (1984). Home safety: Development and validation of one component of an ecobehavioral treatment program for abused and neglected children. *Journal of Applied Behavior Analysis, 17*(2), 159–174. https://doi.org/10.1901/jaba.1984.17-159

Trocme, N. (1996). Development and preliminary evaluation of the Ontario child neglect index. *Child Maltreatment, 1*(2), 145–155. https://doi.org/10.1177/1077559596001002006

Watson-Perczel, M., Lutzker, J. R., Greene, B. F., & Mcgimpsey, B. J. (1988). Assessment and modification of home cleanliness among families adjudicated for child neglect. *Behavior Modification, 12*(1), 57–81. https://doi.org/10.1177/01454455880121003

Yantz, C. L., & McCaffrey, R. J. (2009). Effects of parental presence and child characteristics on children's neuropsychological test performance: Third party observer effect confirmed. *The Clinical Neuropsychologist, 23*(1), 118–132. https://doi.org/10.1080/13854040801894722

CHAPTER SEVEN

Multicultural Considerations in Assessment

As in all aspects of human services, multicultural considerations are important for delivering appropriate, high quality treatment. Unfortunately, the social sciences are haunted by an imperialistic past (Connell, 2008). These disciplines were founded on the idea of the 'expert' and the 'other.' In this vein, the doctor or researcher was thought to embody the standard for normalcy and view patients, other cultures, and people different from himself as an object of study. At the time, the standard set for what is normal and acceptable was based on white, Western, patriarchal traits and values. These ethnocentric descriptions became the ideals and the point of comparison for every other culture, practice, emotional expression, and behavior, deeming anything unlike the ideal as a deviation or inferiority (Connell, 2008). Only in the postmodern era are the notions of people or cultures once deemed as inferior valued for their unique wisdom.

The social sciences' commitment to multiculturalism is an ever-evolving journey. Theories, protocols, diagnoses, treatments, and instruments are largely adapted to fit other cultures because they were rooted in and normed on white Western values. To this date, many social science research studies are dominated by samples of White subjects. Because of this, we are left with a dearth of information on the experiences of non-white people (Connell, 2008). A better route would be to ground theories, protocols, instruments, and treatments in a multicultural foundation, rather than adapt what was normed on white Westerners to the rest of the population. Alas, providers still have to work within existing models as we continue to incorporate multicultural voices and research into the body of knowledge on child maltreatment and assessment. Cultural disparities and bias remain problems in assessment. Additionally, LGBTQ people present their own unique considerations as they comprise a culture within itself, and often face discrimination because of cultural values. Providers must approach all assessments with an understanding of cultural issues and how they affect families.

RACE, CULTURE, AND ETHNICITY

The terms race, culture, and ethnicity all refer to different constructs but are often used interchangeably in the social sciences. Culture refers to a set of values, beliefs, practices, and acceptable behaviors inherent to a certain group. This word does not refer to countries but to any group of people, including friend groups and professional settings. When we refer to culture in the social sciences, we are typically referring to ethnic culture. Ethnic culture is the culture of one's ethnicity of origin and includes worldview, collective knowledge and ways of understanding, interpersonal behaviors, healing practices, traditions, language, dress, food, and child-rearing practices. A person's ethnic culture influences their ethnic identity and their identity as a whole. Cultures are fluid and can change over time, and people are not homogenous within their cultures. People in the same family can express their culture in different ways as well (Fontes, 2005). Providers should consider how culture affects someone's presentation without stereotyping them based on a monolithic understanding of their culture of origin.

Race is a term used to reference people with similar physical biological characteristics like skin color or hair texture, and sometimes a shared geographical origin. Some researchers argue that race is not synonymous with culture because groups of people can be of the same race but have different values, attitudes, and practices (Gershoff & Grogan-Kaylor, 2016). While the term race does not adequately portray the variations in culture within a race, people within a race do share at least some experiences. For example, Black people in the United States share a history of slavery, disenfranchisement, and discrimination. These shared experiences can mean Black Americans constitute a culture though their ethnic cultures can vary within (Fontes, 2005; Gershoff & Grogan-Kaylor, 2016).

BIAS IN ASSESSMENT

Bias is prevalent in many fields and areas of society and is particularly detrimental to child maltreatment risk assessment. Biases can be both explicit and implicit. Explicit biases are overt dislikes and negative attitudes toward a certain group of people. Implicit biases, on the other hand, are attitudes and beliefs that are largely out of a person's awareness. The schemas people have about race, ethnicity, and gender can lead to perpetuating discrimination without intention (Payne et al., 2017). Even the most competent and culturally aware people have implicit biases as no one can help but absorb information from the society in which they were raised. One study found that counselors seldom held explicit biases but frequently held implicit biases, even when they self-evaluated as being highly culturally competent (Boysen, 2009).

Bias is formed through stereotypes, or generalizations about groups of people. Stereotypes exaggerate the variance between people from different groups and the similarities of people within the same group. Stereotypes can be negative, positive, or neutral. Positive stereotypes ascribe positive qualities to people from the same racial or ethnic group but are still damaging because they still assume sameness based on skin tone or ethnicity. Stereotypes are learned in societies through families, peer groups, organizations, and the media. Ironically, providers can also form stereotypes through multicultural awareness trainings, in which they assume that people are homogenous within a culture (Fontes, 2005) or by confusing stereotypes with expertise. Providers that have incomplete information about families are more likely to operate on stereotypes (Berger et al., 2005).

Some label bias in human services as metacolonialism, or a revival of colonial oppression and discrimination that imposes one, typically Western, worldview on everyone (Bulhan, 2015). Allowing bias in assessment is not only unethical, but many studies found it leads to an increase in false positives and false negatives. For example, providers have been found to rate physical abuse as more likely in Black families, resulting from racial stereotypes on parenting, while overlooking abuse in white families, resulting from the stereotype that abuse is more common in families of color (Lane et al., 2002). Black newborns are also more likely to be tested for drug exposure than white newborns (Chasnoff et al., 1990). Another study found that Black mothers who were interviewed by white providers were less likely to receive positive ratings than white mothers interviewed by white providers. Additionally, Black providers seemed to rank both white and Black mothers equally (Berger et al., 2005). Children and families can behave differently when observed by providers from a different racial or ethnic group than their own (Berger et al., 2005) and Black children were found to score lower on cognitive tests when tests were administered by white proctors rather than Black proctors (Kim et al., 2003).

Bias can occur at every level in the child welfare system, from screening and reporting, to assessment and intervention. The legal and court systems pose further risks for bias once a family becomes involved with the system. Black families and families of color are more likely to come into contact with mandated maltreatment reporters, and are more likely to be reported for potential maltreatment, even when none is present (Berger et al., 2005). Substantiation of maltreatment allegations is also more likely for these demographics, even when case characteristics match those in cases where maltreatment was not substantiated. Bias can also occur in decisions to remove children from or return them to their homes (Berger et al., 2005). Providers should work to become aware of their biases by reflecting on their perceptions, ethnocentrism, and their own cultural worldviews.

CULTURAL DISPARITIES IN CHILD WELFARE

Black families and families of color are overrepresented in the child welfare system at every level from reporting to intervention. This disparity can be seen in child maltreatment reporting, the frequency services are provided, and in the demographics of the foster care system. In the United States, Black children make up less than 20% of the general population (US Census Bureau, 2018) but represent 23% of the children in foster care (US Department of Health and Human Services, 2019). In Texas, Black children were removed from their homes at a lower risk threshold than white children (Rivaux et al., 2008). One study found that Black and Latino toddler-age children were more likely to receive skeletal surveys for physical abuse and more likely to be reported for maltreatment than white children of the same age group, even after controlling for insurance status and likelihood of maltreatment (Lane et al., 2002).

Though Black children and children of color are not more likely to be abused or neglected than white children, disparities in the child welfare system persist. Researchers attribute this overrepresentation to poverty and bias. Economic disadvantage and neighborhood instability are major risk factors for abuse and neglect. More people of color live below the poverty line and in impoverished neighborhoods and, therefore, can be at greater risk for maltreatment, or contact with the child welfare system, because of contextual factors (Berger et al., 2005). Bias is thought to be a primary reason for the overrepresentation of people of color in the child welfare system (Berger et al., 2005; Nadan et al., 2015; Najdowski et al., 2020). Stereotypes about parenting and on what constitutes a deviation from the norm can lead to bias in decision making, leading to systemic disparities. Particularly in the medical field, stereotypes about Black parents engaging in intergenerational violence persist (Najdowski et al., 2020). Decision making, especially in medical fields, is often done under time and resource constraints. In these cases, providers are more likely to rely on stereotypes, even implicitly, to make their decisions, leading to increased false positives and false negatives (Najdowski et al., 2020).

THE MULTICULTURAL ECOLOGICAL MODEL

Child maltreatment risk factors must be viewed in the context of a child's ecology. The interplay of factors within the child, within the immediate family, within the community, and within society at large must be considered when evaluating risk. This view is based on Bronfenbrenner's (1979) ecological model of human development. Detailed further in Chapter 5, Bronfenbrenner includes the microsystem or child's immediate family, the mesosystem or interactions between levels, the exosystem or greater community, and the macrosystem or societal values at large. Belsky (1980) expanded on this model in the child maltreatment literature with ontogenic factors, or factors within the individual.

Several researchers have argued that the ecological model must take into account factors associated with culture and immigration (Cicchetti & Valentino, 2006). A parent's cultural context influences parenting attitudes and child rearing beliefs and practices, and parent factors influenced by culture can affect a child's environment. For example, a parent's immigrant status might affect their ability to obtain adequate employment. The parent's personal stress over this issue and the resulting financial strain can both be risk factors for maltreatment.

Fontes (2005) amends the Bronfenbrenner model to incorporate culture. In this model, levels include the individual child, the child's home and family, ethnic culture, proximal social systems, and wider social systems. Individual child factors include the child's genetics, development, and experiences; ethnic culture refers to the family's ethnicity and culture; proximal social systems refer to neighborhoods, schools, and peer groups; and wider social systems refer to legislative policies (Fontes, 2005). Fontes states this culturally oriented ecological framework can help providers become aware of the multiple levels of intervention available. This framework can also take into account the roles of families and communities in individual outcomes, a focus that centers on collectivistic cultures rather than making Western culture the default. This model also helps providers understand their role in the child's ecology. The ethnicity of the provider, and social forces the provider faces, are also influences in a child's life (Fontes, 2005).

THE INTERSECTIONAL PERSPECTIVE

People can be affected by being members of more than one culture or group simultaneously. Crenshaw (1989) first defined the term intersectionality to address the concerns of Black women. Crenshaw and contemporaries argued that Black women were misrepresented in feminist groups because they suffered both gender-based and race-based oppression. Since then, intersectionality theory has expanded to include intersections of age, ethnicity, sexual orientation, socioeconomic status, disability, religion, and other social positions. Intersectionality theory posits that numerous social positions can be experienced simultaneously and that these positions cannot be evaluated singularly. Rather, they should be evaluated in terms of the compounded effects of social stressors (Nadan et al., 2015).

Applied to the ecological model, intersectionality can help explain variables at the macro and micro levels, as well as the interaction between these variables. At the macro level, intersectionality explains how structural discrimination affects the individual. At the micro level, intersectionality explains how individuals personally experience their identities, bias, and discrimination (Syed, 2010). Moreover, intersectionality theory teaches providers that intersecting identities, and the way they influence multiple levels of development, should be considered together.

STRESSORS ASSOCIATED WITH CULTURE

Culturally and ethnically diverse people can experience multiple, compounding stressors that increase the likelihood of maltreatment and act as barriers to receiving care. Stressors can include acculturative stress, exploitation, immigration status, family separation, unequal power systems, discrimination, and posttraumatic stress. Ethnic and racial minorities are more likely to face economic insecurity, residential segregation, and fewer educational and vocational opportunities (Miller et al., 2010).

Immigrant parents face acculturation challenges and might be at a different acculturation level than their children, increasing both personal stress and parenting stress. Immigrant parents face not only acculturative stress, but also higher rates of marital conflict and financial difficulties (Yoo, 2019). Some immigrants might be refugees and may have faced ethnic conflict, war, exploitation, and human trafficking. In a survey of Arab American immigrant and refugee women, 43.9% had been exposed to combat or had been in a war zone (Kulwicki & Ballout, 2015). In the United States, most victims of human trafficking are female immigrants (Human Rights Center & Free the Slaves, 2004). Victims of human trafficking often endure physical abuse, psychological abuse, sexual assault, and food and sleep deprivation (ACLU, n.d.). People who are trafficked are forced into labor with paltry or no compensation and many are forced into sexual slavery (ACLU, n.d.).

Immigration itself presents a stressor. Some immigrants arrived in the US without proper documentation and face deportation and limited access to employment and resources. Immigrants who arrived this way may also have come through human smuggling, a process through which people who are paid a bounty smuggle people across the United States border. Those who engaged in human smuggling are more likely to have experienced physical abuse and sexual assault (US Department of Justice, 2016). Families can also be separated through the immigration process. Some are forced to leave family members behind, some lose family members to violence or exploitation, and some are detained separately if caught arriving at the United States border without going through proper channels (Binensztok & Vastardis, 2019).

Ethnically and racially diverse people often face discrimination in the United States. Discrimination can be overt in the form of insults and persecution, covert in the form of implicit bias, or systemic in the form of employment, financial, or legal discrimination. Discrimination, acculturative stress, experiences of ethnic violence in the homeland, human trafficking, and human smuggling all place ethnic and racial minorities, particularly immigrants, at higher risk for posttraumatic stress (Kulwicki & Ballout, 2015). One study found that rates of posttraumatic stress disorder were three times higher in Latina immigrant women than women in the United States as a whole (Cleaveland & Frankenfeld, 2019).

LGBTQ CONCERNS IN CHILD MALTREATMENT

The intersection between child maltreatment, culture, and LGBTQ concerns is threefold. First, LGBTQ youth are at higher risk of maltreatment and family rejection. Second, LGBTQ people face cultural challenges as a sexual minority, and third, LGBTQ status and ethnic culture can intersect in ways that increase risk of maltreatment. When working with LGBTQ youth, providers must be aware of the ways that LGBTQ identity and ethnic culture intersect and influence risk of child maltreatment. See Figure 7.1 for the intersection of LGBTQ status, culture, and maltreatment.

LGBTQ YOUTH AND MALTREATMENT

LGBTQ people report having experienced childhood maltreatment, including both physical and psychological abuse, at higher rates than non-LGBTQ people (Corliss et al., 2002). LGBTQ youth are more likely to enter the child welfare system and more likely to experience family rejection (Friedman et al., 2011). Within the child welfare system, LGBTQ youth report higher levels of suicidal ideation, suicide attempts, and depression (Scannapieco et al., 2018). Family rejection can also lead to homelessness, with LGBTQ youth reporting homelessness at a rate 120 times higher than their non-LGBTQ peers (University of Chicago, n.d.). A larger number of LGBTQ youth in the child welfare system

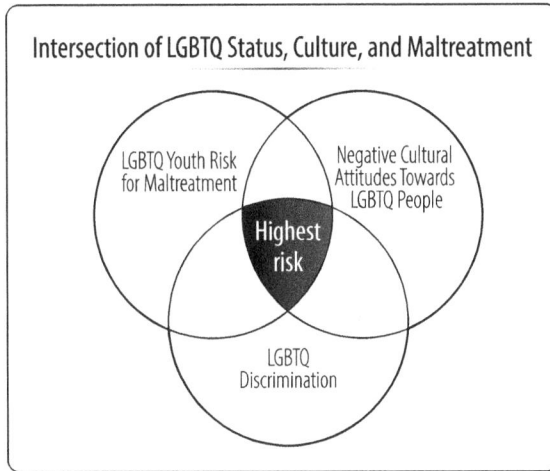

Figure 7.1 Intersection of LGBTQ Status, Culture, and Maltreatment

have reported being thrown out of their homes, homelessness spanning over one year, childhood maltreatment, mental health problems, and further victimization while homeless than non-LGBTQ youth (Forge et al., 2018). Youth who identify as LGBTQ are also less likely to be adopted or reunited with their families than non-LGBTQ youth (Jacobs & Freundlich, 2006). Transgender youth face particularly harsh challenges and resulting mental health symptoms. In one study, the majority of transgender respondents reported being called disparaging names by their parents because of their gender identity or presentation (Grossman et al., 2005).

LGBTQ YOUTH AS A SEXUAL MINORITY

LGBTQ people constitute a culture within themselves and face minority status and other cultural challenges. LGBTQ youth are more likely to experience abuse at not only the hands of their caregivers, but also peers and other adults (Alessi et al., 2016). These experiences can lead to increased incidence of mental health conditions. Because LGBTQ youth are at greater risk for homelessness, they are, as a result, at greater risk for sex trafficking and substance use disorders (Fong & Berger Cardoso,

2010; Forge et al., 2018). School environments can be particularly hostile for LGBTQ youth. Bullying and harassment are commonplace for many LGBTQ youth, resulting in higher rates of truancy (Craig et al., 2018). Teachers can also be biased or prejudiced toward LGBTQ people, leading to an unsupportive school environment that fosters peer victimization (Craig et al., 2018).

INTERSECTION OF LGBTQ AND ETHNIC CULTURE

People in some cultures and ethnicities can hold harmful views about LGBTQ people that put children in this demographic at higher risk for maltreatment. Most cultures, including Western cultures, have historically been prejudiced against LGBTQ and gender non-conforming people. In line with intersectional theory, youth who are both LGBTQ and cultural or ethnic minorities face discrimination for both identities. These youth are referred to as 'double minorities' (Boykin, 1997), as they face both LGBTQ-based discrimination and ethnically based discrimination. A study of Chinese LGBTQ youth found that respondents identified an experience of 'double rejection' (Chiang et al., 2018).

While the United States has more recently progressed in terms of affording rights to LGBTQ people, this demographic still faces discrimination and oppression in both the United States and globally, with some countries making same-sex relationships illegal. Around 80 countries have some legislation against LGBTQ people, and those who engage in same-sex relationships also face violence from civilians (Lovell, 2015). Same-sex relationships are criminalized in places like Nigeria, Uganda, and the Middle East, and in countries like Russia where being LGBTQ is illegal, it might still be socially pathologized (Alessi et al., 2016). In these countries, anti-LGBTQ violence is culturally fueled (Lovell, 2015) and can also manifest as abuse of LGBTQ-identified children.

There are many reasons why cultures can hold discriminatory beliefs toward LGBTQ people. For some, religious beliefs might condemn

LGBTQ people. Some scholars suggest colonial histories contribute to intolerance. In parts of the Caribbean, where same-sex relationships are denigrated and criminalized, homophobia is best understood as a result of British colonialism as people often view same-sex relationships as a white man's perversion, resulting from a history of slaves experiencing sexual assault, including same-sex assault (Lovell, 2015). LGBTQ youth of Asian, African, Middle Eastern, Eastern European, Latin American, and Caribbean origin reported experiencing verbal, physical, and sexual abuse in childhood and adolescence. Abuse was experienced at home, school, and in the community. These youth also cited having no protective resources and experiencing mental health symptoms like depression, anxiety, and suicidal ideation (Alessi et al., 2016). Culture can also interfere with the disclosure of abuse for LGBTQ youth. Several studies have pointed to lower rates of reporting of sexual abuse in multicultural families, attributed to factors like shame, family honor, homophobia, and virginity prizing (Fontes, 2005; Xu & Zheng, 2015).

Negative cultural attitudes toward transgender children can be particularly harmful. Though the ideas of being transgender, dual gender, or third gender were common in some cultures, particularly those in Southeast Asia, views toward gender non-conforming people have taken a negative turn. At one point, Southeast Asian religions were dualistic, in that they incorporated male and female elements equally. In many cases, religious figures would take on gender non-conforming appearances. For the South Sulawesi people of Indonesia, the *bissu* were male ritualists who donned female dress and could engage in same-sex relations. These figures were viewed as nobility (Peletz, 2006). The *sida-sida* were priests in the pre-Islamic Malay Peninsula, who presented in an androgynous fashion as well (Peletz, 2006). In India, the hirjas represent a third gender, recognized by law, of people assigned male at birth who dress in feminine clothing and accoutrements (Dutta, 2012).

Sadly, reverence of gender-nonconforming people has turned to discrimination in many cultures. Anthropologists trace cultural transphobia back through colonialism. Peletz (2006) writes that Spanish colonialists decried cultural ideas of a female shaman as Satanism. Shamanism was considered inherently male and the confluence of male and female elements was labeled a sin. Even in Indian cultures, where a third gender is recognized, attitudes toward youth who identify as transgender were found to be moderately negative (Elischberger et al., 2017). In cultures of hypermasculinity, transgender youth are more likely to experience maltreatment (Elischberger et al., 2017). For minority youth, family rejection and violence because of gender or sexual identity are cited as the primary reasons for homelessness (Durso & Gates, 2012).

MULTICULTURAL ASSESSMENT CONSIDERATIONS

Multicultural considerations in assessment include considerations of how assessments are conducted, cultural barriers to assessment, and determination of what constitutes harm within a cultural context. When asking questions, choosing instruments, and evaluating data, providers should incorporate an understanding of how culture affects the family being evaluated. First, providers should be aware that rapport-building and interviewing can look different with clients of different cultures and ethnicities. With multicultural clients, client comfort, demeanor, expectations, and language barriers should be taken into consideration. In some cases, providers might have to work with translators to conduct clinical interviews. Culture can also influence the quality of information gathered. Culture can affect if abuse is disclosed, whether parents view an act as abusive, and the expression of psychological symptoms.

INTERACTING WITH FAMILIES

Completing a fair and effective assessment requires building adequate rapport with families. To build rapport with multicultural families, providers should be aware of cultural values, communication styles, and language. For some families, the definition of who constitutes a family varies. A Western-centric provider might envision a typical family unit as a nuclear family, consisting of two parents and their children. For culturally diverse families, however, the family structure can include parents, step-parents, grandparents, aunts, uncles, and other extended family. All family members might be seen as equal in contribution and caregiving responsibilities. Fontes (2005) recommends interviewing all people the family identifies as being part of the unit.

Cultural values also include hierarchies, expectations of respect, and use of eye contact in communication. Many cultures value a hierarchy in the family unit. Hierarchies can be in terms of age, status, or gender. In some cultures, it is customary to greet the male elder of the family first while in others it is customary to first greet the female family elder (Fontes, 2005). Using more formal salutations can be helpful when first greeting family members. Providers should also keep in mind that people of different cultures can vary in their use of eye contact. For example, one study found that people from East Asian cultures tended to perceive faces as angry and unpleasant when direct eye contact was made compared to people from Western Europe (Akechi et al., 2013). The direction of the gaze, whether direct or averted, was also found to influence people's perceptions about another's mood or presentation (Akechi et al., 2013).

Providers should also consider the meeting location. All evaluations should ideally be completed in neutral environments. The definition of a neutral environment might differ, however, for people of varying cultures (Fontes, 2005). Some children might feel comfortable at school, while others do not. Children should help identify a safe place where they feel comfortable completing interviews. They should be allowed to bring along toys or anything else they find comforting (Fontes, 2005). Families might choose to meet at schools, worship centers, community resource centers, or other locations they feel are familiar and neutral to them. If police have to be present, this should be handled delicately as people from minority groups can distrust the police (Fontes, 2005). Seating arrangements and physical proximity should also be considered to increase clients' comfort.

LANGUAGE BARRIERS

For some clients, language might be an obstacle to assessment. If someone in the family does not speak English, a provider who speaks their native language should be assigned to the case. When that is not possible, a translator can be used. Providers should be aware that translators can bring another set of challenges. Being evaluated for child maltreatment or risk for maltreatment can place stress on any family, and families who are ethnic, racial, and cultural minorities can face even greater stresses, stemming from histories of being subjected to stereotyping, bias, and discrimination. Some families might already be distressed about allowing a stranger into their family and the use of a translator adds yet another foreign observer to the situation. When using a translator, clients will not only have to become comfortable with providers but translators as well (Fontes, 2005).

In the case that an interview is conducted in the family's native language, a skilled translator should still interpret the interview into English so that crucial data and nuances are not lost. Some children and families might communicate in more than one language or might say most things in English but communicate certain ideas in their native language as there might not be equivalent translations or clients might not know the translations (Fontes, 2005). In these cases, it is helpful to note what is said and employ the use of a translator to discern what the client was trying to communicate. Additionally, people of different ethnicities can communicate through nonverbal expression as well. It is helpful for the provider to become familiar with facial expressions, hand gestures, and other nonverbal expressions.

Another language barrier arises in the use of standardized instruments. Many instruments are not translated into other languages, or enough languages, to be useful for all families. Some instruments, like the Adverse Childhood Experience scale and the Parenting Stress Index – Short Form are translated into Spanish. A number of other useful measures, like the Beck Depression Inventory, are translated to Spanish as well. This still leaves out many instruments and many other languages. It might be a struggle to find useful instruments in other languages. Additionally, even those instruments translated to other languages may be culturally bound. Validation studies ensure that translations convey accurate messages and maintain the integrity of the instruments, but these instruments are still constructed from Western-centric concepts.

Few instruments are created through a multicultural lens and normed on multicultural populations. One such instrument, the Immigrant Parental Stress Inventory (IPSI) (Yoo & Vonk, 2012), addresses stress experienced by immigrant parents within the context of their culture and language. This 33-item self-report instrument was normed on Korean immigrant parents and distinguishes between the stress of immigrant life and the stress of acculturative gaps between parents and children. Another instrument, the Mexican Parenting Questionnaire (MPQ) (Halgunseth & Ispa, 2012) is a 14-item self-report instrument for Mexican immigrant mothers of children age six to ten. This instrument is based on qualitative interviews with Mexican immigrant mothers. Still, there is a lack of instruments rooted in multiculturalism and constructed on qualitative information about multicultural families. Providers should choose the most culturally sound and language-accessible instruments for the families with which they are working.

DISCLOSURE OF ABUSE

Cultural factors can affect the usefulness of the information gathered in an evaluation. One way this can happen is when cultural values interfere with abuse reporting and disclosure. Families of varying cultures might be hesitant to disclose abuse for reasons including shame, taboo, honor, or patriarchy. Collectivistic cultures value group cohesion, which can suppress disclosure of abuse within a family (Xu et al., 2018). Value of family harmony is seen in Chinese culture where maltreatment can be seen as shameful, leading to secrecy (Xu et al., 2018). Within these cultures, shame can prevent children and adult family members from acknowledging or disclosing sexual abuse in particular (Back et al., 2003).

Cultural and religious taboos can instill shame in children and keep them from disclosing. Families might worry about how they will be perceived by other family members, friends, neighbors, and members of the community. Views about family honor, pride, and virginity can also stand in the way of disclosure of sexual abuse, and family hierarchical structures that place males at the top can silence victims and other family members (Fontes & Plummer, 2010). In Asian cultures, an emphasis on collectivism, filial piety, and not displaying emotions can explain unwillingness to disclose sexual abuse (Elliott & Urquiza, 2006). From the Confucian tradition, filial piety emphasizes respect for one's elders.

VIEWS ON PARENTING AND ABUSE

Culture can influence views on parenting and discipline. Views on corporal punishment can be particularly variable between cultures. Corporal punishment can be seen as acceptable and even helpful in many cultures. In Caribbean cultures, Asian cultures, Latin American cultures, and others, corporal punishment can be viewed as an effective tool. One study found that Cambodian parents were more likely to hold positive views on corporal punishment but also have different standards for raising boys and girls (Nho & Seng, 2017). Though most legal definitions use physical marks as an indicator of abuse, other physical punishments are more difficult to assess (Fontes, 2005).

Parental intent does not effectively mitigate the effects of disciplining practices, like corporal punishment, as discussed further in Chapter 2. Yet beliefs about what constitutes abuse vary and can impede disclosure and reporting of physical abuse. Parents might simply not report abusive acts because they do not view them as abusive. Providers should also take cultural beliefs on discipline into account when evaluating what constitutes abuse and if a child is at risk for abuse.

Still, providers should not use culture as an excuse for maltreatment (Fontes, 2005; Kolhatkar & Berkowitz, 2014) and should remember that people are not homogenous within their cultures (Cyr et al., 2013).

While culture can influence parenting views and beliefs, it is not the sole influencing factor. Personal factors, like personality, and external factors, like social support, can influence people as much as culture and influence how culture affects people. All culturally relevant information should be considered within the family's environment and context (Cyr et al., 2013).

SYMPTOM EXPRESSION

Culture can affect assessment and information gathering because of how people display symptoms and how symptoms are interpreted. Providers often have to evaluate psychological and behavioral symptoms as they align with diagnoses when identifying maltreatment and assessing risk for maltreatment. For ethnoculturally diverse clients, however, symptoms might be culturally appropriate and, therefore, not attributable to a mental health diagnosis (American Psychiatric Association, 2013). Rogler et al. (1994) describe Puerto Rican men's expressions, or idioms of distress, as feelings of anger and injustice. In other cases, people from some cultures can express mental health syndromes through somatic symptoms. People from Asian cultures can be more likely to express somatic symptoms and describe their mental health symptoms in somatic terms (Choi et al., 2016).

Symptoms of transgenerational trauma can also complicate symptom assessment in children (Binensztok & Vastardis, 2019). Transgenerational trauma is sometimes referred to as historical trauma, multigenerational trauma, or collective trauma, and encompasses symptoms of trauma that are passed down through generations where family members experienced significant trauma, like ethnic violence. Children of holocaust survivors who were diagnosed with posttraumatic stress disorder (PTSD) were found to be at greater risk for PTSD themselves (Yehuda et al., 2018). Symptom expression correlating to trauma within generations is often attributed to epigenetic changes, altered parental stress responses, social modeling, and parenting behaviors affected by trauma (Yehuda et al., 2018). The way children display symptoms can be affected by these factors. Still, some researchers caution against locating specific types of symptoms too narrowly within cultures as context. The nature of any underlying mental health conditions can affect presentation, making it difficult to determine the function of behaviors (Kirmayer et al., 2017).

BECOMING CULTURALLY COMPETENT

All assessments should be done through a multicultural lens and providers should refrain from making assumptions about families based on perceived culture, race, or ethnicity. First impressions are subject to influence from the provider's existing schemas and implicit biases. Additionally, culture should not be assumed. Rather, the provider should use interviewing and qualitative methods to understand a family's culture and ethnicity. Providers are not expected to be thoroughly familiar with every culture and ethnicity. Cultural competence requires a commitment to flexibility and continuous learning. Culturally competent providers will approach each family with an open mind and learn about new cultures they encounter. Providers can educate themselves about cultures and ethnicities foreign to them by reading about a particular culture, consulting with experts, and listening to the family themselves. Providers should particularly strive to learn and understand how culture influences child-rearing practices and parenting attitudes. Cultural awareness can also help providers approach families with respect and build effective rapport.

Providers should gather all pertinent information about a case before forming conclusions, as lack of information has been correlated with biased decision making in multicultural families in the child welfare system (Berger et al., 2005). Providers should also reflect on their own biases and beliefs. Tools like the Implicit Association Test (IAT) help identify implicit biases (Project Implicit, n.d.). Made available online by Harvard University, the IAT tests implicit bias by showing the respondent a series of images where the respondent must determine if a person possesses a particular quality or not (i.e. dangerous, aggressive). Respondents are asked to answer quickly, and the test determines if the results indicate respondent association of negative traits with race, culture, age, or gender.

Research on cultural adaptations of evidence-based treatments can be helpful in guiding providers in their assessment work as well. Evidence-based treatments that are culturally adapted demonstrated increased effectiveness with ethnically and racially diverse clients than did non culturally adapted treatments (Santa-Sosa & Runyon, 2014). The ecological validity model provides a framework for understanding how ethnocultural factors affect treatment (Bernal et al., 2009). This model emphasizes using the client's preferred language, aligning the family's and provider's ethnocultural background, and the provider's knowledge of the client's cultural values, beliefs, and metaphors. Both providers and agencies should work on continuously improving cultural competence through learning, self-reflection, and honoring cultural factors at every stage of the assessment process.

CASE STUDY 1

Tammy, an eight-year-old female of Middle Eastern descent, informed her school nurse that one of her uncles touched her 'in a bad place.' The nurse made an abuse report to the local child welfare agency and investigators struggled to substantiate the sexual abuse allegations. The investigation report stated that Tammy did not have any physical injuries or marks. Though Tammy reiterated to the investigator that her uncle had touched her inappropriately, the family denied this. Tammy's mother told the investigator that Tammy is 'just making trouble' so she can go to a sleepover at her friend's house. Child welfare workers found that different extended family members, and sometimes friends, stay at the family's home and that the uncle had been staying with them. The uncle was made to leave the home and Tammy's parents were instructed to not allow him back in the home or around Tammy by himself. Both of Tammy's parents are immigrants and, while her mother speaks English more fluently, her father still struggles with English, though he can speak enough to work at his job as a tollbooth worker. Tammy and her family live in a neighborhood with many immigrants of Middle Eastern, Latino, and Southeast Asian descent. Tammy has two siblings – a six-year-old female and three-year-old male.

CASE STUDY 1 DISCUSSION PROMPTS

1. As the provider, list what you would need to know about this family before beginning an assessment.
2. Describe how the family's culture influences the way the assessment will be conducted.
3. Explain your concerns for risk for sexual abuse in this case.

CASE STUDY 2

Stephen is a 14-year-old male of Caribbean descent. Both of Stephen' parents are immigrants from the Caribbean. Stephen tells his school counselor that his parents caught him watching a movie about a young man coming out to his family as LGBTQ and accused Stephen of being gay. Stephen states he is gay, and he is exploring what that means and that is why he was watching the movie but that he denied being gay to his parents because 'they don't approve of that kind of stuff.' Stephen reports that his parents believe being gay 'isn't a thing' and that it 'just means you are not praying hard enough or living clean enough.' Stephen reports that though he denied being gay, his father still hit him with a belt after catching him watching the movie and that his mother is making him pray every day. Stephen states his family worries that he will 'live a sinful lifestyle' and that he will sully their family name. Stephen says he plans to tell his parents that one of his female friends is his girlfriend and that she has agreed to play along. He believes this will satisfy them and decrease the tension in the household. Stephen asks the counselor not to speak to his parents about this situation. He says his parents 'rarely' spank him and that otherwise they are 'really good parents.' He states he likes living at home and that his parents 'make a lot of sacrifices for me and my sister. They work really hard.'

CASE STUDY 2 DISCUSSION PROMPTS

1. List the risk and protective factors in Stephen's family that are apparent in this case study.
2. Describe how culture affects your perception of whether or not Stephen is at risk for maltreatment.
3. Describe how to best approach this case and Stephen's parents.

SUMMARY

This chapter distinguished between race, ethnicity, and culture. Bias in assessment and racial and ethnic disproportionality in the child welfare system was discussed. A multicultural version of the ecological model was presented, and stressors faced by multicultural families were explored. LGBTQ concerns were discussed, particularly the intersection of LGBTQ people's risk for maltreatment and cultural views of LGBTQ people. Considerations for assessment, like client rapport, use of translators, and understanding symptom expression were presented along with suggestions for increasing cultural competence.

REFERENCES

Akechi, H., Senju, A., Uibo, H., Kikuchi, Y., Hasegawa, T., & Hietanen, J. K. (2013). Attention to eye contact in the west and east: Autonomic responses and evaluative ratings. *PLoS ONE, 8*(3), e59312. https://doi.org/10.1371/journal.pone.0059312

Alessi, E. J., Kahn, S., & Chatterji, S. (2016). 'The darkest times of my life:' Recollections of child abuse among forced migrants persecuted because of their sexual orientation and gender identity. *Child Abuse & Neglect, 51,* 93–105. https://doi.org/10.1016/j.chiabu.2015.10.030

American Civil Liberties Union. (n.d.). *Human trafficking: Modern enslavement of immigrant women in the United States.* ACLU.

American Psychiatric Association. (2013). *Diagnostic and statistical manual of mental disorders* (5th edn). APA.

Back, S. E., Jackson, J. L., Fitzgerald, M., Shaffer, A., Salstrom, S., & Osman, M. (2003). Child sexual and physical abuse among college students in Singapore and the United States. *Child Abuse & Neglect, 27*(11), 1259–1275. https://doi.org/10.1016/j.chiabu.2003.06.001

Belsky, J. (1980). Child maltreatment: An ecological integration. *American Psychologist, 35*(4), 320–335. https://doi.org/10.1037/0003-066x.35.4.320

Berger, L., McDaniel, M., & Paxson, C. (2005). Assessing parenting behaviors across racial groups: Implications for the child welfare system. *Social Service Review, 79*(4), 653–688. https://doi.org/10.1086/454389

Bernal, G., Jiménez-Chafey, M. I., & Domenech Rodríguez, M. M. (2009). Cultural adaptation of treatments: A resource for considering culture in evidence-based practice. *Professional Psychology: Research and Practice, 40*(4), 361–368. https://doi.org/10.1037/a0016401

Binensztok, V., & Vastardis, T. E. (2019). Child abuse assessment strategy and inventories. In L. Sperry (Ed.), *Couple and family assessment: Contemporary and cutting-edge strategies* (3rd edn). Routledge.

Boykin, K. (1997) *One more river to cross: Black & gay in America.* Anchor Books.

Boysen, G. A. (2009). A review of experimental studies of explicit and implicit bias among counselors. *Journal of Multicultural Counseling and Development, 37*(4), 240–249. https://doi.org/10.1002/j.2161-1912.2009.tb00106.x

Bronfenbrenner, U. (1979). *The ecology of human development: Experiments by nature and design.* Harvard University Press.

Bulhan, H. A. (2015). Stages of colonialism in Africa: From occupation of land to occupation of being. *Journal of Social and Political Psychology*, *3*(1), 239–256. https://doi.org/10.5964/jspp.v3i1.143

Chasnoff, I., Landress, H., & Barrett, M. (1990). The prevalence of illicit-drug or alcohol use during pregnancy and discrepancies in mandatory reporting in Pinellas County, Florida. *International Journal of Gynecology & Obstetrics*, *33*(4), 389–389. https://doi.org/10.1016/0020-7292(90)90575-6

Chiang, S. Y., Fleming, T., Lucassen, M. F., Fouche, C., & Fenaughty, J. (2018). From secrecy to discretion: The views of psychological therapists on supporting Chinese sexual and gender minority young people. *Children and Youth Services Review*, *93*, 307–314. https://doi.org/10.1016/j.childyouth.2018.08.005

Choi, E., Chentsova-Dutton, Y., & Parrott, W. (2016). The effectiveness of somatization in communicating distress in Korean and American cultural contexts. *Frontiers in Psychology*, *7*. https://doi.org/10.3389/fpsyg.2016.00383

Cicchetti, D., & Valentino, K. (2006). An ecological-transactional perspective on child maltreatment: Failure of the average expectable environment and its influence on child development. In D. Cicchetti & D. J. Cohen (Eds.), *Developmental psychopathology: Risk, disorder, and adaptation*. Wiley. https://doi.org/10.1002/9780470939406.ch4

Cleaveland, C., & Frankenfeld, C. (2019). 'They kill people over nothing': An exploratory study of Latina immigrant trauma. *Journal of Social Service Research*, *46*(4), 507–523. https://doi.org/10.1080/01488376.2019.1602100

Connell, R. (2008). *Southern theory*. Allen & Unwin Epz Titles.

Corliss, H. L., Cochran, S. D., & Mays, V. M. (2002). Reports of parental maltreatment during childhood in a United States population-based survey of homosexual, bisexual, and heterosexual adults. *Child Abuse & Neglect*, *26*(11), 1165–1178. https://doi.org/10.1016/s0145-2134(02)00385-x

Craig, S. L., McInroy, L. B., & Austin, A. (2018). 'Someone to have my back': Exploring the needs of racially and ethnically diverse lesbian, gay, bisexual, and transgender high school students. *Children & Schools*, *40*(4), 231–239. https://doi.org/10.1093/cs/cdy016

Crenshaw, K. (1989). Demarginalizing the intersection of race and sex: A black feminist critique of antidiscrimination doctrine, feminist theory, and antiracist politics. In *Legal Forum*. University of Chicago.

Cyr, C., Michel, G., & Dumais, M. (2013). Child maltreatment as a global phenomenon: From trauma to prevention. *International Journal of Psychology*, *48*(2), 141–148. https://doi.org/10.1080/00207594.2012.705435

Durso, L. E., & Gates, G. J. (2012). *Serving our youth: Findings from a national survey of services providers working with lesbian, gay, bisexual, and transgender youth who are homeless or at risk of becoming homeless.* UCLA: The Williams Institute.

Dutta, A. (2012). An epistemology of collusion: Hijras, kothis, and the historical (dis)continuity of gender/sexual identities in eastern India. *Gender & History*, *24*(3), 825–849. https://doi.org/10.1111/j.1468-0424.2012.01712.x

Elischberger, H. B., Glazier, J. J., Hill, E. D., & Verduzco-Baker, L. (2017). Attitudes toward and beliefs about transgender youth: A cross-cultural comparison between the United States and India. *Sex Roles*, *78*(1–2), 142–160. https://doi.org/10.1007/s11199-017-0778-3

Elliott, K., & Urquiza, A. (2006). Ethnicity, culture, and child maltreatment. *Journal of Social Issues*, *62*(4), 787–809. https://doi.org/10.1111/j.1540-4560.2006.00487.x

Fong, R., & Berger Cardoso, J. (2010). Child human trafficking victims: Challenges for the child welfare system. *Evaluation and Program Planning*, *33*(3), 311–316. https://doi.org/10.1016/j.evalprogplan.2009.06.018

Fontes, L. A. (2005). *Child abuse and culture: Working with diverse families.* The Guilford Press.

Fontes, L. A., & Plummer, C. (2010). Cultural issues in disclosures of child sexual abuse. *Journal of Child Sexual Abuse*, *19*(5), 491–518. https://doi.org/10.1080/10538712.2010.512520

Forge, N., Hartinger-Saunders, R., Wright, E., & Ruel, E. (2018). Out of the system and onto the streets: LGBTQ-identified youth experiencing homelessness with past child welfare system involvement. *Child Welfare*, *96*(2), 47–74.

Friedman, M. S., Marshal, M. P., Guadamuz, T. E., Wei, C., Wong, C. F., Saewyc, E. M., & Stall, R. (2011). A meta-analysis of disparities in childhood sexual abuse, parental physical abuse, and peer victimization among sexual minority and sexual nonminority individuals. *American Journal of Public Health*, *101*(8), 1481–1494. https://doi.org/10.2105/ajph.2009.190009

Gershoff, E. T., & Grogan-Kaylor, A. (2016). Race as a moderator of associations between spanking and child outcomes. *Family Relations*, *65*(3), 490–501. https://doi.org/10.1111/fare.12205

Grossman, A. H., D'Augelli, A. R., Howell, T. J., & Hubbard, S. (2005). Parents' reactions to transgender youths' gender nonconforming expression and identity. *Journal of Gay and Lesbian Social Services, 18*, 3–16.

Halgunseth, L. C., & Ispa, J. M. (2012). Mexican parenting questionnaire (MPQ). *Hispanic Journal of Behavioral Sciences, 34*(2), 232–250. https://doi.org/10.1177/0739986312437010

Human Rights Center, Univ. of California, Berkeley & Free the Slaves. (2004). *Hidden slaves: Forced labor in the United States.* https://humanrights.berkeley.edu/publications/hidden-slaves-forced-labor-united-states

Jacobs, J., & Freundlich, M. (2006). Achieving permanency for LGBTQ youth. *Child Welfare, 85*(2), 299–316.

Kim, H., Baydar, N., & Greek, A. (2003). Testing conditions influence the race gap in cognition and achievement estimated by household survey data. *Journal of Applied Developmental Psychology, 23*(5), 567–582. https://doi.org/10.1016/s0193-3973(02)00142-9

Kirmayer, L. J., Gomez-Carrillo, A., & Veissière, S. (2017). Culture and depression in global mental health: An ecosocial approach to the phenomenology of psychiatric disorders. *Social Science & Medicine, 183*, 163–168. https://doi.org/10.1016/j.socscimed.2017.04.034

Kolhatkar, G., & Berkowitz, C. (2014). Cultural considerations and child maltreatment. *Pediatric Clinics of North America, 61*(5), 1007–1022. https://doi.org/10.1016/j.pcl.2014.06.005

Kulwicki, A., & Ballout, S. (2015). Post-traumatic stress disorder (PTSD) in Arab American refugee and recent immigrant women. *Journal of Cultural Diversity, 22*(2), 9–12.

Lane, W. G., Rubin, D. M., Monteith, R., & Christian, C. W. (2002). Racial differences in the evaluation of pediatric fractures for physical abuse. *JAMA, 288*(13), 1603–1609. https://doi.org/10.1001/jama.288.13.1603

Lovell, J. S. (2015). 'We are Jamaicans:' Living with and challenging the criminalization of homosexuality in Jamaica. *Contemporary Justice Review, 19*(1), 86–102. https://doi.org/10.1080/10282580.2015.1101687

Miller, K. M., Gil-Kashiwabara, E., Briggs, H. E., & Hatcher, S. (2010). Contexts of race, ethnicity, and culture for children of incarcerated parents. In J. M. Eddy & J. Poehlmann (Eds.), *Children of incarcerated parents: A handbook for researchers and practitioners.* The Urban Institute Press.

Nadan, Y., Spilsbury, J. C., & Korbin, J. E. (2015). Culture and context in understanding child maltreatment: Contributions of intersectionality and neighborhood-based research. *Child Abuse & Neglect, 41*, 40–48. https://doi. org/10.1016/j.chiabu.2014.10.021

Najdowski, C. J., Bernstein, K. M., & Waher, K. (2020). Racial stereotyping and misdiagnosis of child abuse: Stereotypes that link race and child abuse may cause medical practitioners to suspect abuse when it hasn't occurred, and to miss it when it has. *Monitor on Psychology, 51*(5), 35–36.

Nho, C., & Seng, T. (2017). Predictors of Cambodian parents' perceptions of corporal punishment. *Asian Social Work and Policy Review, 11*(2), 168–180. https://doi.org/10.1111/aswp.12123

Payne, B., Vuletich, H. A., & Lundberg, K. B. (2017). The bias of crowds: How implicit bias bridges personal and systemic prejudice. *Psychological Inquiry, 28*(4), 233–248. https://doi.org/10.1080/1047840x.2017.1335568

Peletz, M. (2006). Transgenderism and gender pluralism in Southeast Asia since early modern times. *Current Anthropology, 47*(2), 309–340. https://doi.org/ 10.1086/498947

Project Implicit. (n.d.). *Implicit Association Test.* Harvard University.

Rivaux, S. L., James, J., Wittenstorm, K., Baumann, D., Sheets, J., Henry, J., & Henries, V. (2008). The intersection of race, poverty, and risk: Understanding the decision to provide services to clients and to remove children. *Child Welfare, 87*, 151–168.

Rogler, L. H., Cortes, D. E., & Malgady, R. G. (1994). The mental health relevance of idioms of distress, anger and perceptions of injustice among New York Puerto Ricans. *The Journal of Nervous and Mental Disease, 182*(6), 327–330. https://doi.org/10.1097/00005053-199406000-00003

Santa-Sosa, E. J., & Runyon, M. K. (2014). Addressing ethnocultural factors in treatment for child physical abuse. *Journal of Child and Family Studies, 24*(6), 1660–1671. https://doi.org/10.1007/s10826-014-9969-5

Scannapieco, M., Painter, K. R., & Blau, G. (2018). A comparison of LGBTQ youth and heterosexual youth in the child welfare system: Mental health and substance abuse occurrence and outcomes. *Children and Youth Services Review, 91*, 39–46. https://doi.org/10.1016/j.childyouth.2018.05.016

Syed, M. (2010). Disciplinarity and methodology in intersectionality theory and research. *American Psychologist, 65*(1), 61–62. https://doi.org/10.1037/ a0017495

University of Chicago. (n.d.). *Missed opportunities: Youth homelessness in America.* https://voicesofyouthcount.org/brief/national-estimates-of-youth-homelessness/

US Census Bureau. (2018). *The black alone population in the United States.* www.census.gov/data/tables/2018/demo/race/ppl-ba18.html

US Department of Health and Human Services, Administration for Children and Families, Administration on Children, Youth, and Families, Children's Bureau. (2019). *The AFCARS report.* www.acf.hhs.gov/cb/report/afcars-report-26

US Department of Justice. (2016). *Foster youth 2016 statistics yearbook.* www.justice.gov/eoir/page/file/fysb16/download

Xu, Y., & Zheng, Y. (2015). Prevalence of childhood sexual abuse among lesbian, gay, and bisexual people: A meta-analysis. *Journal of Child Sexual Abuse, 24*(3), 315–331. https://doi.org/10.1080/10538712.2015.1006746

Xu, Y., Bright, C., & Ahn, H. (2018). Responding to child maltreatment: Comparison between the USA and China. *International Journal of Social Welfare, 27*, 107–120. https://doi.org/10.1111/ijsw.12287

Yehuda, R., Lehrner, A., & Bierer, L. M. (2018). The public reception of putative epigenetic mechanisms in the transgenerational effects of trauma. *Environmental Epigenetics, 4*(2). https://doi.org/10.1093/eep/dvy018

Yoo, S. Y. (2019). The impact of immigrant parental stress on the risk of child maltreatment among Korean immigrant parents. *Journal of Child & Adolescent Trauma, 12*(1), 49–59. https://doi.org/10.1007/s40653-017-0173-9

Yoo, S. Y., & Vonk, M. (2012). The development and initial validation of the immigrant parental stress inventory (IPSI) in a sample of Korean immigrant parents. *Children and Youth Services Review, 34*(5), 989–998. https://doi.org/10.1016/j.childyouth.2012.01.049

CHAPTER EIGHT

The Adequate Parent

Many families, including those in which maltreatment is not present, can possess a number of risk and protective factors. The presence of risk factors, themselves, does not predict risk of harm. Risk factors merely indicate that some variable within a family is associated with increased risk. How does a provider determine if a family who faces many challenges is still providing adequate care to their children? What is the level of functioning a family must demonstrate to be deemed low risk? Providers run the risk of making subjective judgments at this stage of assessment, after all information has been gathered. Therefore, they must be able to compare information about a family, including functioning, risk factors, and protective factors, to a specific standard. Yet, how does one determine such a standard without imposing subjective values?

Views on parenting not only vary between cultures but also change over time within the same cultures. Even within the United States, views on parenting have evolved significantly over time. This modern time period has witnessed a shift toward ideal parenting. Parents are expected to provide their children with the very best and ensure their children have access to every opportunity possible. Yet ideal parenting is not the standard for good parenting. Access to resources like finances, material items, childcare, extracurricular activities, tutoring, etc. should not be held as the standard of good parenting. Instead, researchers have proposed applying what Budd (2005) refers to as minimal parenting standards when completing risk assessments. Using these standards allows families to be evaluated fairly, yet there is still a lack of information on what constitutes minimal parenting standards. This text proposes the concept of the adequate parent, based on the theoretical underpinnings of minimal parenting standards, Winnicott's good enough mother, the Beavers Systems Model of Family Functioning, and Gottman's good enough marriage. This chapter explores these ideas along with the progression of social views on parenting.

PROGRESSION OF SOCIAL VIEWS ON CHILDHOOD AND PARENTING

Sociocultural views on childhood have changed quite dramatically over time. Scholars have traced attitudes toward childhood back through history, discovering that the notion of childhood being a happy and enriching time is a rather modern idea with historical views characterizing children as inherently evil or as disposable property. Though there are always differences between individual families, acts of infanticide and exposure, or leaving an infant in the wilderness to die, were practices seen in societies spanning back to ancient Greece and ancient Rome (Dekker et al., 2012). Changes in views on children as valuable individuals who require nurturing can mostly be connected to the progression in understanding of cognitive development. As children were no longer seen as property, and were increasingly seen as people who needed guidance and education, societies put greater emphasis on schooling and discipline. This led to the more modern view of childhood as a time of nurturing and changed expectations of parenthood.

The scholar DeMause labeled six childrearing modes, or attitudes, across history. These are the infanticide mode ranging up to the 4th century CE, the abandonment mode spanning the 4th century to 13th century, the ambivalent mode spanning the 13th to 17th century, the intrusive mode in the 18th century, leading to the socialization mode starting in the 19th century, and finally to the helping mode from the mid-20th century onward (DeMause, 1974). These modes are marked by dominant schools of thought in these eras, spanning patriarchal family structures, Christian beliefs of original sin, reactions to political ideologies, and scientific discoveries on social and cognitive development.

DeMause's infanticide and abandonment modes reflect periods when children were considered property and patriarchal family structures allowed parents to do as they pleased with children. In these families, fathers could decide to expose a child, or abandon it in the wilderness, particularly in the case of infants with disabilities or birth defects. Though the actual prevalence of infanticide and exposure in societies like ancient Greece is debated, writings, including mythology and work by Plato and Aristotle, mention infanticide, exposure, or destruction of a child (van N. Viljoen, 1959). Aristotle wrote of exposing infants with deformities, while Plato made mention of infants being condemned or destroyed, which some scholars have interpreted to refer to exposure, as a form of birth control or in situations in which families deem infants should not be reared (Rosen, 2005; van N. Viljoen, 1959).

Philosophical, theological, political, and psychological influences on the understanding of human development align with DeMause's ambivalent and intrusive modes. Jenks (2005) refers to two views of childhood that have spanned both time and cultures – the Dionysian child and the Apollonian child. The Dionysian child was viewed as inherently evil, wild, and troublesome. This view was largely shaped by the Christian idea of original sin, an innate state of sinfulness. In this view, children were not seen as innocent but, rather, needing to acquire innocence through outside intervention. This was achieved through baptism until the Protestant Reformation, after which baptism was no longer an option for acquiring innocence for non-Catholic children. This shift placed the responsibility for making children innocent, virtuous, and moral onto parents (Smith, 2011). Aries (1962) viewed this shift as one that marked childhood as its own unique domain. Dionysian parenting relies on adults' strict control over children, often including physical force. Dionysian parenting enforces rigid social order and values with no room for flexibility or individuality (Smith, 2011). In the Dionysian model, the paternal role is of greatest importance with fathers bearing the responsibility for producing well-behaved, moral children.

In contrast, The Apollonian child is viewed as inherently innocent or angelic (Jenks, 2005). While the Dionysian view tended to dominate old European child-rearing practices, the Apollonian view informed the modern Western idea of childhood. Apollonian parenting also places an emphasis on social order, but one that is more informed by industrialization, in which individuality is prized above common social values (Jenks, 2005). Apollonian views gave rise to a child-centered model of parenting, in which a child is allowed to have more agency and develop their own interests. The Apollonian model moves importance from paternal control to maternal nurturing. While Apollonian parenting emphasizes child-centered socialization with the aim of producing well-adjusted individuals, the Apollonian child is still expected to be seen but not heard (Jenks, 2005).

In the 17th century, John Locke wrote of the *tabula rasa*, or the idea that children were born a blank slate, needing to be molded by external influence, rather than just small adults, as they were viewed in the Middle Ages (Larcher; 2015; Locke, 1690). This spurred a move not only away from the Middle Ages' understanding of children but also toward an Aristotelian view of child development that stresses children's need for nurturing, guidance, and support from adults (Larcher, 2015). Soon, the new Enlightenment ushered in an era in which children were viewed as future citizens that needed to be reared and educated. This bore the movement toward compulsory education (Dekker et al., 2012). In Western Europe, the idea of the criminal child was introduced, with separate programs and prisons created for children who committed crimes. At the same time, Enlightenment views progressed beyond the idea of *tabula rasa* and toward an understanding of children having their own internal tendencies and agency in addition to needing external guidance (Dekker et al., 2012).

In the 20th century, psychologists contributed to the understanding of child development that requires empathy and affection on the part of the parent. While children who did not perform well socially or in school were once seen as defective, they were now increasingly seen as products of their environments. Bowlby's (1969) theory of attachment and Piaget's (1939) theory of cognitive development informed how children, childhood, and parent responsibilities were viewed. The idea that children must learn through schooling and parent responses aligns with DeMause's socialization mode and somewhat with Jenks' (2005) Apollonian child model. Smith (2011) proposes the concept of the Athenian child as the model succeeding the Apollonian model. The Athenian model views children similarly to the Apollonian model, stressing child agency and a more democratic parenting process, but deviates from the Apollonian idea that children be separate from the adult world. The Athenian model, which more closely aligns with current Western parenting ideals, emphasizes children's choice and the need for children to communicate their preferences, thoughts, and emotions (Smith, 2011). Here, the child is seen as a partner in their own socialization process. This idea reflects DeMause's helping mode, and Dekker et al. (2012) write of the notion of childhood happiness as a construct only emerging in the mid to late 20th century. These ideas marked a movement away from authoritarianism in parenting and education and toward the consideration of children's agency and emotions. Some scholars view the 1960s movement to educating children to be happy as a societal repudiation of fascism (Dekker et al., 2012).

Though views of children and childhood have evolved in children's favor and currently focus on the emotional, educational, and social wellbeing of children, many scholars point out that the current Western standard of childrearing is one tied to the middle- to upper-middle-class ideals of the late 20th century onward. The average American parent spends more money and more time on parenting than at any time in history (Miller, 2018). Evolving from the mid-20th century idea of child-centered parenting, what is referred to as intensive parenting involves parents focusing all of their energy into making sure their children have the best resources and opportunities (Ishizuka, 2019; Miller, 2018; Valentine et al., 2019). Parents are now focused on expensive extracurricular activities and time-consuming ventures like making homemade baby food. While these parenting acts are not harmful to children and can be greatly enriching, they are largely only available to more affluent families who have not only greater financial resources but also more time and assistance.

The Industrial Revolution intensified expectations on mothers as men increasingly worked outside of the home and mothers were increasingly expected to be all-encompassing nurturing providers (Valentine et al., 2019). These parenting ideals can place great pressure on parents to achieve a standard of perfection and intensive parenting can increase the divide between children of the affluent and children of the working class (Miller, 2018; Valentine et al., 2019). Even parents with ample resources can struggle to meet these parenting ideals and much of the information on parenting presented in the media is culture, race, class, and gender bound (Valentine et al., 2019). As views of parenting change, ideal parenting styles that are limited by resources and finances should not be held as the standard for all parenting.

TOWARD AN UNDERSTANDING OF ADEQUATE PARENTING

It would be unreasonable to expect all parents to conform to one style of parenting, particularly one that is considered ideal. Parenting has evolved to be seen as a complex and delicate task that requires excessive resources and ample skills and can be done a singular correct way (Valentine et al., 2019). In reality, parenting has many variations as families face differing circumstances. Even best practices in parenting may be out of reach for some parents, considering their social and financial resources. Living situations, childcare options, access to medical care, and access to enriching opportunities can vary vastly for families of different socioeconomic status. Parents might live with disabilities or be forced to work long hours or provide less nutritious food to children. This does not mean their parenting is abusive or neglectful.

Ethnocultural factors also influence parenting views and practices, contributing to more variance between families. Many argue that families are unfairly scrutinized for not adhering to inaccessible forms of parenting. The most ethical way to evaluate families is to focus on the idea of the adequate parent. The adequate parent meets the child's basic physical, social, emotional, and developmental needs while protecting the child from harm and not causing the child harm. The concept of adequacy, or being good enough, appears in various areas of the literature on family and couple relationships. D. W. Winnicott (1965) first raised the idea of the good enough mother as a figure who was imperfect but still effective. The Beavers Systems Model of Family Functioning uses the idea of the adequate family as one that is not ideal but still functional. Marital family researcher John Gottman spoke to the idea of the good enough relationship, in which one's needs are met effectively though there might still be problems that arise along the way. Budd (2005) wrote of minimal parenting standards in child welfare and parenting evaluations. Minimal parenting standards denote the minimal level of competence necessary to be effective as a parent. These four ideas are highlighted below and point to the existing concept of adequacy, or being good enough, in the literature.

WINNICOTT AND THE GOOD ENOUGH MOTHER

The psychoanalyst D. W. Winnicott introduced the idea of the good enough mother – a mother who met her child's needs but was imperfect, sometimes falling short of ideal parenting (Winnicott, 1965). Winnicott's work focused on the child's external environment, straying from Freud's psychoanalytic theory that innate drives dictate the course of development. Winnicott's theory involved a dialectical relationship between an infant's internal drives and dynamics and external reality. Winnicott viewed childhood and maturation as a road from dependence to independence with children beginning in a stage of absolute dependence on the parent, moving to relative dependence followed by a stage of moving toward independence (Winnicott, 1965).

Winnicott stated that the good enough mother would meet all of a child's needs in a timely and nurturing way when the child was an infant, in the stage of absolute dependence. Later, however, as the child crossed through stages of relative dependence, the good enough mother would provide an adequate environment, yet fail at times. To Winnicott, imperfection on the part of the good enough mother was actually an important part of child development. He postulated that in infancy, the child feels omnipotent as its cries dictate everything the parent does. As the parent becomes less perfect in time, the child learns about the limits of external reality and learns to adapt to the skills needed to be successful (Lee, 1985; Winnicott, 1965). Winnicott wrote that not only is perfection unattainable, good enough parenting is sufficient for successfully raising children (Choate & Engstrom, 2014; Winnicott, 1965).

BEAVERS SYSTEMS MODEL OF FAMILY FUNCTIONING

The Beavers Systems Model of Family Functioning is a model of family functioning informed by the family systems perspective in which functioning is evaluated across two dimensions – family competence and family style. In the Beavers model, the family competence scale refers to five types of families – optimal families, adequate families, mid-range families, borderline families, and severely dysfunctional families (Beavers & Hampson, 2000). Optimal families are seen as the model for good functioning. These families problem-solve more effectively, and are more intimate, respectful of each other, and flexible (Beavers & Hampson, 2000). Mid-range families can function at some level but both parents and children become more susceptible to mental health problems. These families are characterized by power struggles, harsh discipline, and boundary violations. Parents may play favorites or use children as scapegoats (Beavers & Hampson, 2000).

Borderline families struggle to gain stability and often become mired in chaotic struggles for power and domination. In these families, parental units are unstable, and anger and aggression are expressed more frequently. Children in these families are at risk for developing mental health disorders (Beavers & Hampson, 2000). Severely dysfunctional families display chaotic functioning and power is typically displayed indirectly. These families lack intimacy, cohesion, goal-directedness, and communication. Children in severely dysfunctional families are at risk for being delayed in their socioemotional development (Beavers & Hampson, 2000). Positioned between optimal and mid-range families are adequate families, who are more rigid and controlling than optimal families. Adequate families tend to resolve conflict by exerting force. In these families, the parental unit can be strained but still effective. Though these families enjoy less happiness and intimacy than optimal range families, they still can function effectively enough not to put children at the level of risk in mid-range families (Beavers & Hampson, 2000).

GOTTMAN AND THE GOOD ENOUGH MARRIAGE

Leading researcher in couple dynamics and marital therapy John Gottman discussed the idea of the good enough relationship. In his description of the good enough relationship, Gottman (2018) explains that partners in these relationships have high standards for how they wish to be treated but still understand that conflict will occur and that some problems will show up throughout the relationship. Standards for a relationship include love, affection, respect, loyalty, and kindness, and the absence of physical or emotional abuse (Gottman, 2018).

Through years of research, Gottman created the theory of the Sound Relationship House, which outlines the characteristics of good enough relationships. Gottman postulated that good enough relationships are relationships in which couples are good friends, enjoy their sex life, have trust and commitment, constructively navigate conflict, and can repair emotional ruptures in the relationship (Gottman, 2018). Though this idea applies to romantic relationships, it speaks to the notion of being good enough rather than perfect. Good enough still implies that certain standards have to be met but acknowledges that problems and failures will occur but do not necessarily indicate dysfunction in overall relationship functioning.

BUDD AND MINIMAL PARENTING STANDARDS

Adcock and White (1985) brought Winnicott's ideas of good enough parenting into the child welfare sphere when they begged the question of what level of parental functioning should the government deem unacceptable in order to intervene in families. Budd (2005) uses this concept in the realm of parenting evaluations, suggesting the use of minimal parenting standards or competencies. Budd writes that all parents should not be compared to optimally functioning parents. Rather, providers should focus on a parent's ability to meet a child's basic emotional and safety needs. This is referred to as the 'lowest threshold of parenting skills' (Budd, 2005, p. 433). Like many authors, Budd mentions the lack of universal standards or models of minimally acceptable parenting. As a response to this, providers should evaluate families within context and in terms of children's needs. Family risk factors like mental illness or disability can be mitigated by other strengths like the child's level of functioning or the family's level of social support (Budd, 2005). Like the good enough parent, the minimally competent parent is imperfect and may fail at times but is still functional enough to be effective.

ASSESSING ADEQUATE PARENTING

As previously mentioned, though parents should be evaluated according to minimal standards of competence, there is little consensus about what constitutes minimal or adequate parenting. Some state that adequate parenting requires centering the child's needs, consistency, and boundary setting, though these concepts are poorly defined themselves (Taylor et al., 2009). There are no actuarial instruments that assess minimal parenting competence, and assessments can only point to the possible outcomes of unmediated risk factors (Choate & Engstrom, 2014). One study identified four factors associated with adequate parenting. These are meeting the child's health and

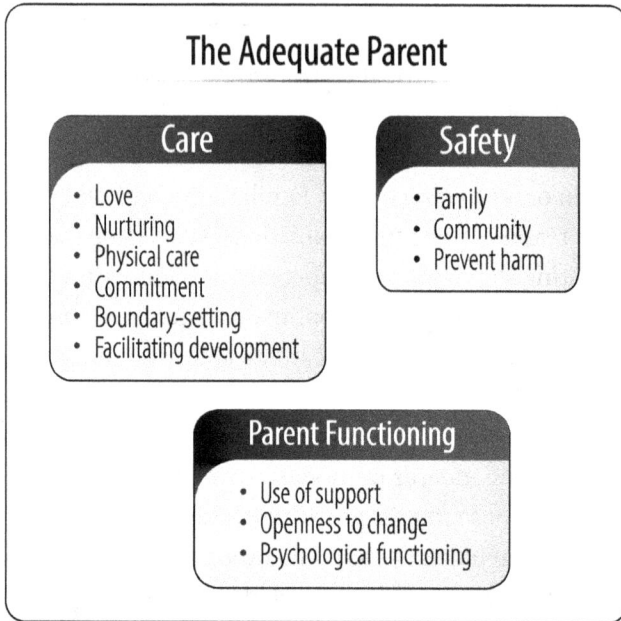

Figure 8.1 *The Adequate Parent*

developmental needs, centering the child's needs, consistency of care, and parent use of external support services (Kellett & Apps, 2009). Other authors posit that adequate parenting is characterized by love, care, commitment, limit-setting, support of development (Hoghughi & Speight, 1998), and meeting the child's physical, emotional, cognitive, and developmental needs (Budd et al., 2011). For the purposes of this text, areas of consideration for assessment of adequate parenting include care, safety, and parent functioning. These domains are explained further below and Figure 8.1 illustrates the domains of the adequate parent.

CARE

Adequate care involves meeting child needs across several domains. Care includes physical care, emotional care or nurturing, love, appropriate boundary setting, and facilitation of development. Budd et al., (2011) stress physical care that includes adequate housing, food, clothing, medical care, and other basic necessities. Hoghughi and Speight (1998) point to love, care, and commitment, emphasizing that children need to feel loved both consistently and unconditionally, fostering a secure attachment between them and their parents. Nurturing requires the parent to be available both physically and emotionally to meet basic needs (Budd et al., 2011). Hoghughi and Speight also stress appropriate boundary and limit setting. Boundary setting in adequate families teaches children about effective behaviors and is flexible, loving, and consistent. Hoghughi and Speight's third factor in adequate parenting is the facilitation of development. The adequate family will provide opportunities to stimulate and foster child cognitive and socioemotional development. Support of child cognitive development requires interaction and appropriate opportunities for the child to grow. Piaget (1939) outlined stages of child cognitive development. These include the sensorimotor stage, the preoperational stage, the concrete operational stage, and the formal operational stage. Parents, and other adults, can play a crucial role in supporting cognitive development through their interactions with children and the opportunities they provide to children (Larcher, 2015). Table 8.1 outlines Piaget's stages of cognitive development and how the adequate parent can facilitate development at these stages.

Providers can assess how parents meet children's socioemotional needs based on theories like Erikson's Stages of Psychosocial Development. Erikson (1950) outlined eight stages of human psychosocial development, five of which are completed in childhood and adolescence. These include trust vs mistrust, autonomy vs shame, initiative vs guilt, industry vs inferiority, and identity vs role confusion. Erikson believed that humans face a conflict or a basic question at each stage that determines their future course of development. The way parents respond to children's socioemotional developmental needs can influence self-esteem and identity development (Beyers & Goossens, 2008). Table 8.2 outlines Erikson's stages of development and how the adequate parent can support the child at these stages.

Table 8.1 Piaget's Cognitive Development Stages and the Adequate Parent

Stage	Age	Basic Task	Required Parenting
Sensorimotor	Birth – 24 months	Discovery through senses	Provide stimulating toys and activities Interact with child verbally and physically Respond with appropriate facial and vocal expressions
Preoperational	2–7 years old	Symbolic thinking	Understand that the child sees things from an egocentric perspective Encourage the child to grasp more complex concepts without being punitive Understand that bad or mischievous behavior does not mean a bad or ill-intended child Understand that children this age struggle to connect cause and effect
Concrete Operational	7–11 years old	Concrete thinking	Support child's increased use of logic Reward child for autonomous thought and decisions Set appropriate limits while encouraging reasoning with the child
Formal Operational	12 – adulthood	Abstract thinking	Encourage abstract and hypothetical thinking Help children learn to plan and set goals Support exploration of new ideas

Table 8.2 Erikson's Stages of Psychosocial Development and the Adequate Parent

Stage	Age	Basic Question	Required Parenting
Trust vs Mistrust	Birth – 30 months	Can I trust my caregivers?	Meeting child needs consistently Holding and interacting with the child
Autonomy vs Shame	30 months – 3 years old	Can I gain independence?	Encouraging the child to make small choices Potty training in a supporting/ nonpunitive way
Initiative vs Guilt	3–5 years old	Can I have control over my environment?	Facilitating external relationships Encouraging positive interactions at school Supporting schooling
Industry vs Inferiority	5–12 years old	Can I be proud of myself?	Taking an active role in schooling Participating in child's academic, athletic, and social life
Identity vs Role Confusion	12–18 years old	Can I find my own identity?	Supporting personal exploration Setting appropriate boundaries Facilitating communication Encouraging social relationships Providing insight and information

SAFETY

The adequate parent will make appropriate safety provisions for the child, within their ability. Community safety is not guaranteed, and providers should not rush to determine increased risk if the family lives in an unsafe community or neighborhood, though this is a considerable risk factor for maltreatment. Rather, the provider should determine what the parent does to mitigate the risks in their community (Choate & Engstrom, 2014). If the neighborhood makes it unsafe for children to play outside, the adequate parent will arrange appropriate supervision for children. If crime or gangs threaten the child's safety, the adequate parent will do their best, within their means, to protect the child by using community resources like subsidized aftercare and enrichment programs. Just as important as community safety, the adequate parent will provide family safety. The adequate family will be free of interpersonal and intimate partner violence. Not only is family violence a risk factor for maltreatment and trauma within itself, it can compound other safety factors like community risks.

Still, sometimes incidents occur that are beyond a parent's control. An incidence of violence may occur unexpectedly within the home. Child maltreatment can occur from parents, spouses, significant others, extended family members, and neighbors. If the parent becomes aware of this maltreatment, or risk for maltreatment, the adequate parent will take appropriate steps to prevent harm to the child. For example, if someone physically or sexually abuses the child and the parent learns of or suspects abuse, the parent should be sure to keep this person away from the child, seek necessary medical care, and call law enforcement when merited. Finally, an adequate parent does not perpetuate harm by using excessive or cruel punishment and is sensitive to preventing psychological and emotional harm.

PARENT FUNCTIONING

As previously discussed, a parent's openness to change, use of external resources, and general psychological functioning can all be either risk or protective factors for child maltreatment. Parents who are struggling in some areas can still improve and be adequate parents if they are open to change and implementing suggestions from professionals. Many risk factors can be remediated by changes on the part of the parent. The Stages of Change model (Prochaska et al., 1992) outlines stages of motivation for changing one's life or behavior. These stages of change are precontemplation or denial that a problem exists, contemplation or acknowledging a problem exists but not being ready to address it, preparation or investigating ways a problem can be ameliorated, action or taking active steps to address a problem, and maintenance or maintaining progress made. Families with risk factors that need to be managed who are in the precontemplation stage can be much more difficult to work with than those in preparation or action stages. Being in the preparation or action stages allows for interventions that manage any existing risk factors. Parents who are in the precontemplation or contemplation stages who are flexible enough to move closer to the action stage might also be considered adequate depending on the context.

Adequate parent functioning is also characterized by use of external resources. Adequate parents use their social support networks and the community resources available to them. For example, a parent might be struggling with food insecurity, putting them at higher risk for neglect. If that parent uses resources like food banks and subsidized school lunches, however, they not only compensate for what they lack, but also demonstrate resiliency, flexibility, and openness to change. Use of external resources also models resiliency and a sense of community to children, providing them with tools for increasing wellness (Choate & Engstrom, 2014). External resources can include family, friends, schools, government resources, community centers that provide youth activities or supplies, food banks, and other sources.

A parent's psychological functioning also factors into adequate parenting. Parent substance use disorders and mental health problems can be serious risk factors for maltreatment. This does not mean, however, that the existence of such problems, themselves, deems a parent inadequate. The severity and effect on daily functioning must be taken into account. The way a parent manages mental health problems is important as well. Adequate parents address their mental health concerns without parentifying the child or using the child to ameliorate their personal historical difficulties and traumatic experiences (Budd et al., 2011; Choate & Engstrom, 2014; Reder, 1995). Numerous authors stress not stigmatizing parents with mental health conditions and not imposing ethnocentric views on culturally diverse parents with mental health concerns. Even those with both mental and physical disabilities can function adequately as parents (Choate & Engstrom, 2014; Swain & Cameron, 2003).

CASE STUDY

The Rodriguez family is comprised of a mother and father, three children – Jayden, age two, Sammie, age five, and Veronica, age seven – and the family's maternal grandmother, all of Latino descent. Mr Rodriguez is an immigrant and naturalized citizen while Mrs Rodriguez was born in the United States. The family lives in community subsidized housing in a neighborhood with relatively high rates of both violent and nonviolent crime. In the previous month, there was a drive-by shooting that left a teenager dead, just a few blocks away from the family's residence. The family states they are aware of the violence, but they try to focus on their family, as they cannot afford to live in a different community. No community violence has directly affected the family and though there is some concern about the children playing outside, the family manages this by only allowing the children outside during daylight hours and relying on friends and neighbors to supervise the children.

In the community housing complex, there is a center courtyard and many children play there while parents, aunts, and grandparents from various neighboring families spend time talking in the courtyard and watching all of the children collectively. Both parents in the Rodriguez family work outside of the home. The mother works in housekeeping in an office plaza and the father works as a flooring installer and earns extra money driving for a rideshare service part time. Because the parents both work long hours, they rely on subsidized daycare, aftercare, and activity programs hosted by the local urban youth center. The maternal grandmother also plays a significant role in the childrearing though she has several health problems and often cannot keep up with all three children at once.

Because of recent budget cuts, some of the community programs utilized by the family were diminished or eliminated entirely. Veronica participated in an after school band program that was indefinitely suspended, and Sammie participated in a community martial arts program for children. Supplies were once provided for the program but because of funding constraints, parents became required to purchase uniforms and other necessary supplies. Because the Rodriguez family could not afford to purchase these items, Sammie stopped attending the martial arts program. Since then, both children spend more time at home unsupervised while the grandmother sleeps or is out of the home and the parents work.

On one occasion, Veronica went missing for several hours. The family found the child at a basketball court several blocks away but did not realize she had left the home for several hours. All three children are at a healthy weight and none have medical conditions. The children are up-to-date with their vaccines and regular check-ups but, because of their busy work schedules, the parents rarely attend school functions and parent-teacher conferences. Mr and Mrs Rodriguez share the disciplinary duties. Both parents use time-outs, loss of items or privilege, and spanking as punishments. The children are typically disciplined for fighting with each other or being disobedient. On two occasions, spankings left a bruise on Veronica's buttocks.

Mr and Mrs Rodriguez have reasonable expectations of their children for their developmental ages. They show affection and communicate love for their children. The parents have a loving relationship though they occasionally argue. Most arguments occur when the father occasionally drinks too much. There have been no incidences of physical violence between the parents though they raise their voices, and both have broken a plate or other object on several occasions. The family's home is small, with the two older children sharing a bedroom, the youngest child sleeping in the parents' bedroom, and the grandmother in a private den area. There are no visible hazards but clutter often accumulates. Neither parent has a criminal record but a paternal uncle, who often visits the home, has a felony record for theft and possession of marijuana.

CASE STUDY DISCUSSION PROMPTS

1. Identify the risk and protective factors in the Rodriguez family.
2. Do the parents meet the standards for adequate parenting? Explain your rationale.
3. What services could help the family decrease risk?

SUMMARY

This chapter outlined the characteristics of adequate parents. Progressing societal views on childhood through history were explored and analyzed in terms of how they contributed to modern, Western views on parenting. The concept of adequacy and adequate, or good enough, parents was presented from several theories and approaches. A model for assessing adequate parenting was presented, along with a case study.

REFERENCES

Adcock, M., & White, R. (1985). *Good-enough parenting: A framework for assessment*. Hyperion Books.

Aries, P. (1962). *Centuries of childhood*. Random House.

Beavers, R., & Hampson, R. B. (2000). The Beavers systems model of family functioning. *Journal of Family Therapy, 22*(2), 128–143. https://doi.org/10.1111/1467-6427.00143

Beyers, W., & Goossens, L. (2008). Dynamics of perceived parenting and identity formation in late adolescence. *Journal of Adolescence, 31*(2), 165–184. https://doi.org/10.1016/j.adolescence.2007.04.003

Bowlby, J. (1969). *Attachment and loss, vol. 1: Attachment*. Basic Books.

Budd, K. S. (2005). Assessing parenting capacity in a child welfare context. *Children and Youth Services Review, 27*(4), 429–444. https://doi.org/10.1016/j.childyouth.2004.11.008

Budd, K. S., Connell, M., & Clark, J. R. (2011). *Evaluation of parenting capacity in child protection (best practices for forensic mental health assessments).* Oxford University Press.

Choate, P. W., & Engstrom, S. (2014). The 'good enough' parent: Implications for child protection. *Child Care in Practice, 20*(4), 368–382. https://doi.org/10.1080/13575279.2014.915794

Dekker, J. J., Kruithof, B., Simon, F., & Vanobbergen, B. (2012). Discoveries of childhood in history: An introduction. *Paedagogica Historica, 48*(1), 1–9. https://doi.org/10.1080/00309230.2012.644988

DeMause, L. (1974). *The history of childhood.* Harper.

Erikson, E. H. (1950) *Childhood and society.* Norton.

Gottman, J. (2018). *The truth about expectations in relationships.* The Gottman Institute.

Hoghughi, M., & Speight, A. P. (1998). Good enough parenting for all children – a strategy for a healthier society. *Archives of Disease in Childhood, 78*(4), 293–296. https://doi.org/10.1136/adc.78.4.293

Ishizuka, P. (2019). Social class, gender, and contemporary parenting standards in the United States: Evidence from a national survey experiment. *Social Forces, 98*(1), 31–58. https://doi.org/10.1093/sf/soy107

Jenks, C. (2005). *Childhood* (2nd edn). Routledge. https://doi.org/10.4324/9780203129241

Kellett, J., & Apps, J. (2009). *Assessment of parenting and parenting support need: A study of four professional groups.* Joseph Roundtree Foundation.

Larcher, V. (2015). Children are not small adults: Significance of biological and cognitive development in medical practice. In T. Schramme & S. Edwards (Eds.), *Handbook of the philosophy of medicine.* Springer.

Lee, C. (1985). The good-enough family. *Journal of Psychology and Theology, 13*(3), 182–189.

Locke, J. (1690). *Essay concerning human understanding.* Stanford Encyclopedia of Philosophy. https://plato.stanford.edu/entries/locke/

Miller, C. C. (2018). The relentlessness of modern parenting. *The New York Times,* December 25.

Piaget, J. (1939). *Origins of intelligence in the child.* Routledge.

Prochaska, J. O., DiClemente, C. C., & Norcross, J. C. (1992). In search of how people change: Applications to addictive behaviors. *American Psychologist, 47*(9), 1102–1114. https://doi.org/10.1037/0003-066x.47.9.1102

Reder, P. (1995). The meaning of the child. In P. Reder, S. Duncan, & C. Lucey (Eds.), *Studies in the assessment of parenting*. Routledge. https://doi.org/10.4324/9780203420805

Rosen, S. (2005). *Plato's Republic: A study*. Yale University Press.

Smith, K. (2011). Producing governable subjects: Images of childhood old and new. *Childhood, 19*(1), 24–37. https://doi.org/10.1177/0907568211401434

Swain, P. A., & Cameron, N. (2003). 'Good enough parenting:' Parental disability and child protection. *Disability & Society, 18*(2), 165–177. https://doi.org/10.1080/0968759032000052815

Taylor, J., Lauder, W., Moy, M., & Corlett, J. (2009). Practitioner assessments of 'good enough' parenting: Factorial survey. *Journal of Clinical Nursing, 18*(8), 1180–1189. https://doi.org/10.1111/j.1365-2702.2008.02661.x

Valentine, K., Smyth, C., & Newland, J. (2019). 'Good enough' parenting: Negotiating standards and stigma. *International Journal of Drug Policy, 68*, 117–123. https://doi.org/10.1016/j.drugpo.2018.07.009

van N. Viljoen, G. (1959). Plato and Aristotle on the exposure of infants at Athens. *Acta Classica, 2*, 58–69.

Winnicott, D. W. (1965). *The maturational processes and the facilitating environment*. International Universities Press.

CHAPTER NINE

Decision Making in Child Maltreatment Risk Assessment

Despite the immense progress made in the field of child protection, child maltreatment risk assessment still presents an opportunity for many pitfalls and errors. Decisions intended to be in the best interest of children can still be fraught with biases, value-based judgments, and other factors that affect impartiality. Providers must be aware of the cognitive processes of decision making, including both analytical thinking and intuitive thinking. The value of clinical judgment and expertise should be acknowledged, with providers still striving to make decisions using actuarial methods and analytical thinking. Providers must also be aware of the ethical implications of their decisions and strive to uphold ethical standards in assessment.

DECISION MAKING PROCESSES

Decision making is a complex process, in itself, regardless of context or potential consequences. Cognitive processes like deductive reasoning and use of heuristics often occur outside of one's personal awareness. The more complex a problem is, the more likely it is that decisions will be inconsistent or incorrect. Decisions made using ambiguous information, incomplete information, and under time constraints are less accurate and consistent (Pecora et al., 2013). In child welfare, ambiguity abounds and there is more room to make incorrect decisions. Decision making in this realm includes not only decisions about family interventions, some of which can be very intrusive, but providers are also tasked with making hundreds of small decisions during the assessment process. Providers must decide how to approach a family, which instruments to use, and, perhaps most important, whether or not something is a risk factor and how that risk factor affects a family's overall level of risk. While providers who complete assessments do not make final decisions like whether or not to remove a child from a home, their decisions about what is risky leads to this ultimate outcome. Therefore, providers must understand how decisions are made and practice reflection on their own decision making processes.

In the work pioneered by psychologist Daniel Kahneman, two cognitive systems are identified. These are the intuitive system and the analytic system, or what Kahneman refers to as 'thinking fast and slow,' also the title of one of his texts (Kahneman, 2011). Intuitive decisions rely on mental shortcuts, or heuristics, while analytical decisions involve a more thorough analysis of all available details. Kahneman (2011) classifies two cognitive processing systems – System 1 and System 2. System 1 seeks to make general observations about the environment and helps construct the schemas that form intuitive thinking, while System 2 seeks to answer questions or evaluate situations and constitutes analytical thinking. System 1 observations help form heuristics, or mental shortcuts humans use to evaluate situations and make decisions. Both cognitive systems are useful in their own ways and intuitive thinking helps people make decisions under pressure or time constraints, but are subject to biases and errors because heuristics are often used in situations in which they do not apply. For example, the availability heuristic leads someone to grossly overestimate the possibility of an event if there are readily available examples of similar events that occurred previously. A common example of the failure of the availability heuristic is the misconception that planes are more likely to crash than they are, just because incidents of past plane crashes stand out vividly in people's minds.

Intuitive decision making can be a threat to the validity of risk assessments because it allows for biases, subjective judgment, and irrational conclusions. In maltreatment and risk assessments, providers' experience, heuristics, and personal values can impede accurate decision making (Bartelink et al., 2017). Ambiguity and lack of information increase likelihood of intuitive thinking and these factors are prevalent in risk assessment. Another danger is the possibility of providers developing biased heuristics, leading them to quickly draw incorrect conclusions based on personal or cultural beliefs (Enosh et al., 2019). The provider's personal characteristics, the child's personal characteristics, professional or organizational characteristics, and sociocultural characteristics have all been shown to bias providers' decision making in ambiguous contexts (Enosh et al., 2019).

Despite its drawbacks, intuitive thinking cannot be removed from any form of decision making, and some argue that it is a necessary and helpful part of decision making, if used effectively. Kahneman writes that System 2 thinking automatically initiates System 1 thinking, so that even analytical thinking uses some component of System 1 observation and appraisal. Munro (1999) also writes that it is impossible to completely remove the influence of intuitive thinking. While a systematic approach to gathering and analyzing information is the most preferable approach to risk assessment, clinical expertise is required as well, particularly in complex situations, and expertise often comes in the form of intuitive thinking. Kahneman and other authors also tout the value of intuitive thinking, though Kahneman emphasizes the rate of error from intuitive thinking throughout his body of research.

Another cognitive researcher, Gary Klein, stresses the value of intuitive thinking in expert decisions. While Kahneman points to the fallibility of heuristics and biases, Klein refers to the intuitive processes of experts as a naturalistic decision making approach (Kahneman & Klein, 2009). Klein's work draws on research on chess masters' decision making that showed expert chess players made decisions more quickly than novices and that such experts had memorized between 50,000 to 100,000 patterns they could recognize at just a glance at the board (Chase & Simon, 1973; DeGroot, 1978). This sort of acquired pattern recognition has been documented in expert decision makers across disciplines, including firefighting and nursing (Kahneman & Klein, 2009). These expert decision makers rely on System 1 scanning of information and intuitive judgments based on micro-cues in the environment that they have learned to associate with specific meanings and outcomes through a great deal of experience. Many researchers cite the phenomenon that experts often cannot articulate their decision making processes, though true experts are aware of what they do not know, while non-experts can become overconfident in their knowledge and ability (Kahneman & Klein, 2009). The consensus in much of the cognitive psychology literature and the child protection literature is that intuitive thinking is not only inevitable, but also sometimes useful. Providers must, then, rely on algorithms, actuarial instruments, and strategic methods of assessment as much as possible while also honing their clinical expertise, understanding cases within context, and having metacognition of biases and heuristics (Kahneman & Klein, 2009; Pecora et al., 2013).

Aside from intuitive thinking's potential for bias, other biases have been noted in child protection decision making. Munro analyzed decision making in child protection and found that providers were influenced by confirmation bias and focused on too few details when making decisions. Workers were more likely to focus on facts that were more memorable because they were more vivid. Another study found that providers were influenced by the rule of optimism, or the tendency to view parental behaviors in a positive light. In child welfare cases, the rule of optimism is influenced by cultural relativism and providers' belief in natural love, or the notion that all parents instinctively love, nurture, and protect their children (Dingwall et al., 1983).

Providers can also fall under the bias of defensible decision making, in which a decision can be rationalized as the best one possible when, and because, it is the only feasible decision available (Dingwall et al., 1983). More focus is put on mothers, as they are often viewed as the primary caregivers. By doing so, critical family issues and the influence of family violence are easily overlooked, placing the family in greater danger (Gillingham, 2006). Even though providers are tasked with making decisions that serve the best interests of children, the view of what is best can easily be influenced by provider biases (Enosh et al., 2019). Decision making can also be influenced by the ways agencies and professionals collaborate with one another, yet researchers point to several variables that interfere with collaboration. These include denial of problems, avoidance of problems, projection of feelings or ideas, displacement, rationalization/intellectualization of problems, and deflection of blame (Stroud & Warren-Adamson, 2013). Poor collaboration can fuel biased decision making as providers do not have the opportunity to consult with other experts or seek support at higher institutional levels.

DECISION MAKING MODELS

Completing a risk assessment requires the provider to estimate the risk of future harm to children based on existing information. Numerous assessment frameworks exist and vary in terms of their use of structured information gathering techniques, yet none of these models reaches a consensus on the science behind decision making. As described in Chapter 1, some decision making models are consensus-based, relying on clinical judgment to draw conclusions, while others are actuarial, using standardize instruments and checklists. While actuarial models have been proven to be most valid and reliable, the usefulness of clinical expertise cannot be discounted. The following are risk-assessment models commonly implemented in the United States. These include the ACTION for Child Protection SAFE Model, The Structured Decision Making Model, and the Signs of Safety^{TM} model. These models are most often used by teams and agencies, but their theoretical bases are useful in guiding individual provider decision making as well.

ACTION FOR CHILD PROTECTION SAFE MODEL

The ACTION for Child Protection SAFE Model is a consensus-based model that uses structured assessments of threats of danger, child vulnerability, and the protective factors of the caregivers. This model distinguishes between present danger, or immediately threatening danger, and impending danger, or family conditions that are not presently dangerous but unstable enough that they may become dangerous. This model also includes a solution-focused lens, focusing on safety assessment, safety management, and factors that increase parent protective capacity. This model collects data across six focus areas that include child maltreatment, context of the maltreatment, child level of functioning, general parenting style and ability, parenting discipline style, and adult level of functioning.

STRUCTURED DECISION MAKING MODEL (SDM)

The Structured Decision Making Model (SDM) is an actuarial-based model that uses evidence-based standardized assessment instruments. These tools are designed to foster more accurate and consistent decisions. Some instruments used in the SDM began as consensus-based tools and, over time, information gathered through those tools was tested and used to construct more reliable and valid instruments. The SDM system is designed to address the most high-risk families and reduce the probability of future abuse and neglect by providing targeted services. This model aims to respond to incidents that place children at greatest risk for harm, clarify the threshold for danger, identify children who have a higher probability of maltreatment, and assess the safety of children staying in their homes.

SIGNS OF SAFETY™ MODEL

The Signs of Safety™ Model (Turnell & Edwards, 1999) is a strengths-based actuarial model drawing on a solution-focused framework. This model aims to engage all parties to a case, including children, parents, other family members, and professionals. The goal of this model is to establish working relationships between family members and professionals and use critical thinking to make determinations. This model addresses four main family components: harm, danger and complicating factors, strengths and safety factors, provider and family goals for child safety, and provider safety judgments. Signs of Safety provides practical tools for engaging children in both the risk assessment and safety planning process.

ETHICS AND RISK ASSESSMENT

Providers must keep in mind that evaluation of families can be an intrusive process, leaving many parents and children feeling anxious and uncomfortable. Parents who have not harmed their children may fear false positives and all families can fear the stigmas associated with both mental health evaluation and suspicion of child maltreatment. Parents and families who are being evaluated are also subject to having their homes, behaviors, mental health, etc. held under a microscope. Not only is this unsettling to families, it also places families in a vulnerable position in which factors that might otherwise have been overlooked are now possibly viewed as pathological as seen through a risk assessment lens.

Assessment also creates an imbalance of power, as the provider serves as the expert and the family an object of inquiry whose fate rests on the provider's judgment. Providers have the power to influence the course of someone's entire life if evaluations result in children being removed from the home or receiving services. Identification of risk can be stigmatizing but is often the benchmark for whether or not a family will receive much-needed services (Wilkins, 2015). In some cases, workers were found to manipulate assessment tools to indicate higher risk in order for families to qualify for the services they needed (Wilkins, 2015). While some families may welcome social services that help them thrive, others might be burdened by such services. For example, a working parent who does not have transportation might have to sacrifice time and money to attend a pre-scheduled parenting class. Providers should be aware of how the assessment process is perceived and the possible consequences of assessment. While an ethical assessment will not overlook risk factors simply to help families avoid negative consequences, the influence of those stressors on how families behave and engage in assessment should influence the provider's demeanor, assessment strategy, and understanding of the results of standardized and observational assessment tools.

Two views contribute to debate about ethics in risk assessment – Mill's utilitarianism and Kantian deontology. The philosopher John Stuart Mill wrote that utilitarian ethics focuses on outcomes, rather than the means to the end (Mill, 2006). Utilitarianism's goal is to do as much good, to increase happiness outcomes, and avoid doing harm. A teleological approach, utilitarianism stresses the ways in which we achieve these outcomes matter less than the outcomes themselves. In contrast, the philosopher Immanuel Kant's deontology does not sanction any means to an end. Instead, he stresses the value of human autonomy and the ethics of actions, particularly what he referred to as the Categorical Imperative, or the idea of not behaving in a way that one would not desire to be a universal way of behaving, in which the individual would be subject to being treated in the way he treats others (Kant & Schneewind, 1997).

Some scholars argue that Kant's deontology ultimately approaches utilitarianism in that the means trend towards the end (Forschler, 2013). Both ethical views can be valuable in informing decision making in risk assessment. Providers must focus both on increasing positive outcomes and reducing harm, as well as judging actions fairly, maintaining human dignity, and fostering self-determination through the process. Providers must be aware that they are subject to imposing their own ideas, values, beliefs, and emotions during the assessment and decision making process. The ethical provider is reflective on his or her process and can understand and ethically justify which values were applied and which were put aside in decision making.

Ethical issues arise in child maltreatment risk assessment not only during decision making points where information is ambiguous, but also when providers mistake societal problems for individual deficits. Some scholars believe the reframing of social problems as the consequence of individual behaviors represents a diffusion of responsibility at the government and agency levels (Gillingham, 2006). Accountability is inherent to risk assessment. As it is impossible to absolutely predict or prevent harm to children, both unforeseen events as well as those that could have been prevented will inevitably occur. Accountability inherently influences decision making and providers must not only be aware of their own pressures, but also how institutions handle accountability. Blame put on parents as individuals can serve to maintain social order while absolving institutions and ignoring how structural and social influences ultimately increase risk (Gillingham, 2006).

CONSIDERATION OF CHILDREN'S RIGHTS

Parents have rights to guardianship of their children and to rear and discipline their children as they see fit, so long as they do not abuse their children. Parents have decision making authority over their children and can make choices on their children's behalf. Though its goal is to protect children, child welfare work still seeks to protect parent and family autonomy. Yet, while parents should be evaluated in terms of their adequacy, providers should also be considerate of children's rights. Under the law, children do not have the ability to make major life-altering decisions like where they would like to live, to buy alcohol, or consent to getting married. Developmentally, children do not have the capacity to understand the long-term consequences of their decisions, and must have decisions made for them to preserve their safety. Still, children have human rights, like the right to not be discriminated against for one's race, ethnicity, gender, or sexual orientation, as well as other rights central to childhood.

Feinberg & Aiken (1980) differentiate between rights that belong solely to adults, termed A-rights, rights that belong to both adults and children, termed A-C rights, and rights that belong solely to children, termed C-rights. A-rights refer to the right to choose in terms of whether the family follows a specific religion, the family's political leaning and activity, where they live, which groups they belong to, which schools children attend, etc. Welfare rights, like rights to body integrity and agency, privacy, and healthcare can be categorized as both A-rights and A-C rights. C-rights include the right to necessities that the child cannot procure themselves, like shelter and food, as well as the right to be protected from harm. Some argue that a child also has the right to be loved. Feinberg also raises the notion of the right to grow up and 'rights-in-trust,' or rights that a child deserves because they will eventually grow up to be an adult with full adult rights. These rights are to be guarded by not only parents but the state and institutions as well, and include the right to education and opportunities. Eekelaar (1986) mirrors this with his notion of developmental rights, or the right to opportunity without disadvantage as a child transitions to adulthood.

The United Nations Convention on the Rights of the Child outlines a set of considerations of children's rights referred to as the best interest principle (United Nations, 1989). This principle is reflected in decision making that centers the child's best interests. In some cases, this gives the state the right to remove a child, impose decisions that are not concordant with parents' decisions, or even legally terminate a parent's rights. Views about children's best interests can be biased, however. These views, like most others, can be influenced by personal, cultural, and religious values, leaving room for subjective interpretation. Cultural bias may lead a provider to believe they are acting in the best interests of a child when they are not, and cultural relativism can also sacrifice a child's best interests under the guise of cultural sensitivity. The UN Convention specifies children's rights to encompass basic needs, healthcare, education, and opportunity. It also emphasizes a child's right to be heard. Children's input, in consideration of their developmental age, should be evaluated when determining children's best interests (United Nations, 1989).

BEST PRACTICES IN CHILD MALTREATMENT RISK ASSESSMENT

Providers have much to consider through the assessment process, from the initial encounter with the family to the way information is interpreted and presented. Providers should act ethically and use reflective decision making strategies to reduce bias and increase the accuracy of their judgments. Assessments should be done through a multicultural lens, considering cultural implications throughout the process. Providers should evaluate parents according to adequate parenting standards while still acting in the best interest of children. Providers should also seek to reduce ambiguity in decision making

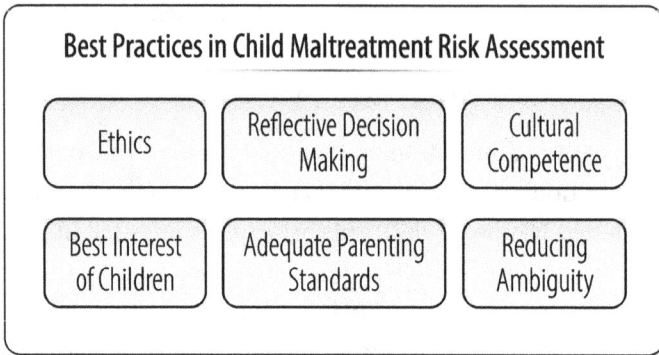

Figure 9.1 *Best Practices in Child Maltreatment Risk Assessment*

and reporting by identifying the scope of the assessment and gathering sufficient and useful information. Figure 9.1 outlines best practices in assessment, which are detailed further below.

ETHICS

Providers completing risk assessments can vary. They can be licensed as counselors, psychologists, or social workers. Provides should abide by the ethical codes of their licensing boards as well as those of their profession's governing body. Furthermore, providers should abide by the ethical standards for forensic family assessment. The Ethical Guidelines for Forensic Psychologists (Committee on Ethical Guidelines for Forensic Psychologists, 1991) can dictate assessment considerations for all providers, regardless of profession. These guidelines state that providers must not serve in multiple roles with a family (i.e. both evaluator and therapist) and must inform families of their rights and responsibilities in assessment. This includes information about the purpose and scope of the assessment and the limits of confidentiality in risk assessment. Confidentiality in risk assessment is much more limited than in other mental health services. Depending on the context of the assessment, multiple people, including lawyers, judges, and other providers, might read the assessment report.

REFLECTIVE DECISION MAKING

Providers should strive to reduce bias and avoid type I and type II errors by accurately interpreting the information they collect. Providers should use actuarial methods, algorithms, and analytical thinking in assessment to reduce bias and intuitive thinking. Additionally, providers must know when to use clinical judgment and expertise in their decision making. Developing a reflective practice can help providers develop expertise and become aware of implicit biases. Reflective practice is stressed in the curricula of many counseling training programs. In one study, counseling students who participated in a guided reflective practice coaching improved their competence in case conceptualization skills more than counseling students who did not participate in such coaching (Binensztok, 2019).

Providers must also focus their decision making by defining the scope of the assessment. The reason for the assessment should be clarified as well as any questions the assessment will and will not answer. Evaluations should answer specific questions about risk and parent functioning but cannot answer questions like whether a child should be removed, or a parent have their rights terminated (Budd, 2005). Providers should be aware of the limitations of assessment. Assessments can only describe parent, child, family, and environmental characteristics and identify strengths, needs, and possible interventions. Assessments should not make broad predictions about parents' behaviors, infer capacity from individual factors like mental health alone, or ignore contextual variables (Budd, 2005).

Providers must also decide what to include in the final report. Reports should specify not only the family's risk and protective factors but also precipitants, perpetuating factors, and targeted interventions that could help the family (Budd, 2005). Furthermore, these factors should not be presented as a disjointed list but, rather, as a cohesive narrative that makes connections between risk, protective, and contextual factors (Pecora et al., 2013). When considering risk factors and possible interventions, researchers stress a shift towards providing parents with support to amplify their strengths and decrease the risk of stressors (Daro, 2019).

CULTURAL COMPETENCE

Providers must continuously work on their cultural competence in order to be fair and effective. It is illogical to assume any provider can possess in-depth knowledge about every ethnicity or culture, so providers should be aware of what they do not know, as much as what they do know, and strive to gain knowledge about the cultures of the clients with whom they are working. They should be aware that people are not homogenous within cultures and avoid using culture as a catchall or creating a biased heuristic based on culture. Clients should be evaluated in their cultural context but also as individuals within their culture. Similarly, providers who are of the same culture or ethnicity as their clients should not assume their experiences are the same or that they can fully understand clients based on the provider's personal cultural experience. Finally, providers must determine not only which factors are attributable to culture, but also whether culture hinders the discovery of abuse and whether to apply relativism or universalism when analyzing if a culturally approved act constitutes maltreatment.

ADEQUATE PARENTING STANDARDS

Parents should be evaluated according to adequate, or minimal, parenting standards rather than optimal parenting standards. Providers must understand that cultural, social, intrapersonal, and economic factors affect family presentation but that parents can still meet their children's needs well enough to raise them safely, even if other challenges exist. Budd recommends a functional approach for parenting evaluations, focusing the evaluation on parental functioning and parent-child interactions rather than individual parent characteristics. Parents should not only be assessed according to standards associated with minimal parenting standards, but reports should also emphasize families' strengths as much as risk factors (Budd, 2005).

Titterton and Taylor (2018) propose a risk and resilience model in which family stressors, adversities, and social conditions serve as risk influencers and are mediated by individual vulnerabilities and resilience processes that can lead to both positive and negative outcomes. Budd (2005) and Pecora et al. (2013) also stress the importance of considering context and environment when assessing parent functioning. Providers should use a template of adequate parenting when making decisions and drawing conclusions but also cogently express their reasoning in a report meant to be used by other providers.

BEST INTEREST OF CHILDREN

In the focus on adequate parenting standards and cultural competence, providers must not forget the primary purpose of all child protection work – to protect children. Parents can have good intentions but still put their children at risk for significant harm. Even in cases where most of the risk factors are outside of parents' control, or the parents are victims themselves, the parents might still pose a risk to the child. Providers can empathize with parents and recommend supportive services in their reports, but should not allow these factors to influence their decisions about level of risk. High-risk families can still openly demonstrate affection for their children and stress their love for their children. Children who are being maltreated can hide abuse, recant their accounts, and express love for parents. While these factors should all be considered along with other data obtained, they do not necessarily decrease the level of risk in a family. Providers should evaluate all information holistically, always using the best interests of children as a guide. While children have limited rights in terms of the law, they still have human rights, the rights to having their basic needs met, the right to opportunity, and the right to be heard.

REDUCING AMBIGUITY

As shown in the research, limited information increases ambiguity, increasing the risk for biased decision making. Providers should strive to reduce ambiguity by using various methods of information gathering for each assessment (Budd, 2005). These can include observations, clinical interviews, standardized tests and instruments, review of records, interviews with collateral sources, and qualitative methods. Observations should be completed in the most naturalistic setting possible, with parents and children observed together (Budd, 2005). Providers can also reduce ambiguity by being clear about the purpose of the assessment and consulting with other providers and agencies. Providers must understand that all decision making contains an element of risk and harm cannot be absolutely predicted or prevented. Providers must also, therefore, become more comfortable with making decisions in ambiguous conditions while decreasing risk for error by using judgement, reflection, and collaboration (Munro, 2011).

CASE STUDY

Kim, a three-year-old female, and Johnny, a five-year-old male, are the children of immigrants from Southeast Asia. The parents are both citizens and the father (33) works in a factory while the mother (29) works at a restaurant. Both parents speak fluent English though it is not their first language, because they immigrated to the United States as teenagers. A risk assessment of the family was ordered after the three-year-old child, Kim, was found wandering on the street alone. She was picked up by a police officer who happened to be driving past. The parents state they lost track of where Kim was because they were engaged in a heated argument. When workers arrived at the home, they discovered some broken glass on the ground around the entrance to the family's first floor apartment. Both children's beds are single mattresses on the floor with cartoon-themed bedding and pillows. Both children are well-nourished and have adequate supplies, clothing, and toys.

The provider completing the assessment conducts clinical interviews with both parents, with each interview occurring over the course of three separate meetings. The provider assesses the home using the Checklist for Living Environments to Assess Neglect (CLEAN). The parents each complete standardized personality testing using the Minnesota Multiphasic Personality Inventory and the following self-report instruments: The Child Abuse Risk Assessment Scale, The Parenting Stress Index – Short Form (PSI-SF), and The Instrument for Identification of Parents at Risk for Child Abuse and Neglect (IPARAN). The provider interviews Johnny, having him draw pictures of his family and create a scene using toys, which the child named 'My family.' The provider conducts observations of parent-child interactions in the home on two separate occasions. The provider reviews the police report from when Kim was found wandering, all caseworker reports, child medical records, and a police report from a domestic disturbance call the family had one year ago. In this report, the provider discovers that neighbors called a noise complaint because of people arguing and the parents were asked to keep it down, but no domestic violence was determined. The provider speaks to collateral sources including case workers, a teacher, a school counselor, daycare workers, and the paternal grandmother, who often helps with the children.

The provider determines both children are well-nourished, in good health, and up-to-date on required medical care. The children seem happy in the home and securely attached to both parents, frequently running back to the parents while playing or asking to be held. The mother is attentive to the children's needs while being observed, with the father not dismissing the children but deferring to the mother for caretaking responsibilities. The primary household responsibilities are managed by the mother as well. Collateral sources indicate that the children seem well-adjusted and have never been observed to have any marks or bruises. The provider consults with a colleague who states it is not uncommon for families to sleep with mattresses on the floor in Southeast Asian cultures and the home, though cluttered, was not untidy and had no visible hazards. Both parents indicated they argue frequently, and Johnny confirmed that the parents often raise their voices. The child did not describe witnessing physical violence in the home. The mother indicated that the father slapped her one time but that is not the norm between them, though they do yell and sometimes the father breaks objects in the home. The parents both stated that their arguments typically involve financial stressors and division of household labor. Though both parents immigrated to the United States as teenagers, they still maintain traditional patriarchal family values.

The provider determines the family's protective factors include a nurturing relationship between the children and parents, the family's use of community daycare and aftercare programs, the adequate provision of basic needs and medical care, the family's willingness to use services, and the support of the maternal grandmother. The family's risk factors include intimate partner violence that is worsened by financial stressors and strict patriarchal values. Substance use, mental health problems, and acculturative stress were not determined to be factors. The parents also work many hours, leaving them drained and less able to take care of their children and more prone to arguing.

The provider determined that though the male being the head of the household with the female partner being more submissive is accepted in the family's culture of origin, it fuels the potential for violence in this case. The provider also determines that the children's risk for neglect seems to be positively correlated to incidents of violence between the parents. The provider deems the family to be at moderate risk for child neglect and moderate risk for intimate partner violence, considering the frequency of their arguments, the perpetuating factors, and the reported infrequency of physical altercations. The provider recommends additional food assistance to the family to ease their financial stressors and recommends a batterer's intervention course for the father and parenting classes for both parents, focusing on the effects of family violence and neglect on children.

CASE STUDY DISCUSSION PROMPTS

1. List the cultural factors that affect the outcome of this case and those that do not affect the outcome.
2. Explain how to weigh the risk factor of intimate partner violence with the protective factor of the nurturing bond between the parents and children in this case.
3. Would your conclusions differ from the provider's in this case? Explain why or why not.

SUMMARY

This chapter explored decision making processes in child maltreatment and their roots in the cognitive psychology research. The usefulness and drawbacks of both intuitive and analytical thinking were discussed along with other factors that complicate decision making in child maltreatment work. The ethics of risk assessment were detailed and guidelines for ethical practice are specified. A discussion of children's rights was followed by an outline of a model for best practices in risk assessment.

REFERENCES

Bartelink, C., de Kwaadsteniet, L., ten Berge, I. J., & Witteman, C. M. (2017). Is it safe? Reliability and validity of structured versus unstructured child safety judgments. *Child & Youth Care Forum, 46*(5), 745–768. https://doi.org/10.1007/s10566-017-9405-2

Binensztok, V. (2019). *The influence of reflective practice on the case conceptualization competence of counselor trainees* [Doctoral dissertation, Florida Atlantic University]. FAU Digital Library.

Budd, K. S. (2005). Assessing parenting capacity in a child welfare context. *Children and Youth Services Review, 27*(4), 429–444. https://doi.org/10.1016/j.childyouth.2004.11.008

Chase, W. G., & Simon, H. A. (1973). The mind's eye in chess. In W. G. Chase (Ed.), *Visual information processing*. Academic Press.

Committee on Ethical Guidelines for Forensic Psychologists. (1991). Specialty guidelines for forensic psychologists. *Law and Human Behavior, 15,* 655–665.

Daro, D. (2019). A shift in perspective: A universal approach to child protection. *The Future of Children, 29*(1), 17–40. https://doi.org/10.1353/foc.2019.0002

DeGroot, A. D. (1978). *Thought and choice in chess*. Mouton.

Dingwall, R., Eekelaar, J., & Murray, T. (1983). *The protection of children: State intervention and family life*. Blackwell.

Eekelaar, J. (1986). The emergence of children's rights. *Oxford Journal of Legal Studies, 6,* 161–182.

Enosh, G., Nouman, H., & Schneck, C. (2019). Child's religiosity, ethnic origin, and gender: A randomized experimental examination of risk assessment and placement decisions in cases of ambiguous risk to children from low SES families. *Research on Social Work Practice, 29*(7), 766–774. https://doi.org/10.1177/1049731518810795

Feinberg, J., & Aiken, W. (1980). A child's right to an open future. In H. LaFollette (Ed.), *Whose child? Parental rights, parental authority, and state power*. Littlefield, Adams, and Co.

Forschler, S. (2013). Kantian and consequentialist ethics: The gap can be bridged. *Metaphilosophy, 44*(1–2), 88–104. https://doi.org/10.1111/meta.12015

Gillingham, P. (2006). Risk assessment in child protection: Problem rather than solution? *Australian Social Work, 59*(1), 86–98. https://doi.org/10.1080/03124070500449804

Kahneman, D. (2011). *Thinking, fast and slow*. Farrar, Straus and Giroux.

Kahneman, D., & Klein, G. (2009). Conditions for intuitive expertise: A failure to disagree. *American Psychologist, 64*(6), 515–526. https://doi.org/10.1037/a0016755

Kant, I., & Schneewind, J. B. (1997). *Lectures on ethics* (P. Heath, Trans.). Cambridge University Press.

Mill, J. S. (2006). *The collected works of John Stuart Mill* (J. M. Robinson, Ed.). University of Toronto Press.

Munro, E. (1999). Common errors of reasoning in child protection work. *Child Abuse & Neglect, 23*(8), 745–758. https://doi.org/10.1016/s0145-2134(99)00053-8

Munro, E. (2011). *The Munro review of child protection: A systems analysis.* The Stationery Office.

Pecora, P. J., Chahine, Z., & Graham, J. C. (2013). Safety and risk assessment frameworks: Overview and implications for child maltreatment fatalities. *Child Welfare, 92*(2), 143–160.

Stroud, J., & Warren-Adamson, C. (2013). Multi-agency child protection: Can risk assessment frameworks be helpful? *Social Work and Social Sciences Review, 16*(3), 37–49. https://doi.org/10.1921/3703160304

Titterton, M., & Taylor, J. (2018). Rethinking risk and resilience in childhood and child maltreatment. *The British Journal of Social Work, 48*(6), 1541–1558. https://doi.org/10.1093/bjsw/bcx117

Turnell, A., & Edwards, S. (1999). *Signs of safety: A solution and safety oriented approach to child protection casework.* W. W. Norton & Company.

United Nations. (1989). *United Nations Convention on the Rights of the Child.* www.unicef.org/child-rights-convention

Wilkins, D. (2015). Balancing risk and protective factors: How do social workers and social work managers analyse referrals that may indicate children are at risk of significant harm. *British Journal of Social Work, 45*(1), 395–411. https://doi.org/10.1093/bjsw/bct114

INDEX

Note: Page numbers in *italics* refer to figures. Page numbers in **bold** refer to tables.

Beck Depression Inventory 156
Behavioral Coding System 126
behavioral problems **48–49**, 50–51, 82
Belsky, J. 100, 123–124, 147
best interest of children 203, 207
best practices, in child maltreatment risk
    assessment 203–208, *204*; adequate
    parenting standards 206–207; ambiguity,
    reducing 208; best interest of children
    203, 207; cultural competence 206; ethics
    204; reflective decision making 205–206
bias, in assessment 144–145
bioecological model 100–101, *101*, 123–124
bipolar disorder 74
bissu 153
borderline families 179
borderline personality disorder 56
boundary setting, in adequate families 183
Bowlby, J. 51–52, 175
brain and nervous structures, affected by
    child maltreatment **47**
Brigid Collins Risk Screener (BCRS) 113
Bronfenbrenner, U. 100, 123, 147
Brunnberg, E. 10
Budd, K. S. 172, 178, 181, 182, 206–207
bullying/harassment 152

Caldwell HOME Inventory for Infants 114
care 182–183, *182*
case study: adequate parenting 188–190;
    assessing families for risk 115–117; child
    discipline method 38; child protective
    services 61; neglect 15; risk/protective
    factors 89–90, 162–163, 208–211; sexual
    abuse 161–162; suspecting forms of
    maltreatment 135–136
Categorical Imperative 201
Centers for Disease Control 58
change, stages of 186–187
Checklist for Living Environments to
    Assess Neglect (CLEAN) 132
child abuse and neglect: from affluent
    families 83–84; cognitive disturbances
    50; conducting assessment of 3–4; death
    and 2; depression and 73; displaying
    emotional and behavioral problems
    50–51, 127; economic disadvantage
    as risk factor for 146; emotional
    disturbances 50; experiencing type II
    traumas 44, 52–53; forms of 23–29,
    28–29, 133; guidelines for prevention
    2; limited training in reporting 3;

multicultural issues and 3; neighborhood
    risk factors 84; neuropsychological
    changes 45; parent attitudes and 76,
    108–109, 124; prior acts of 79; risk of 75;
    symptoms resulting from 120
Child Abuse Potential (CAP) Inventory 113
Child Abuse Prevention and Treatment Act
    of 1974 2
Child Abuse Risk Assessment Scale
    (CARAS) 115
Child Behavior Checklist 128
child-centered parenting 176–177
childhood: happiness 176; and parenting,
    social views on 172–177; psychiatric
    disorders 51
child maltreatment: abandonment 26–27,
    28; accepted cultural practices 34–36;
    ACE study 54–55; adult psychological/
    physical manifestations, of ACE 55–57;
    assessment 101–103, 121; best practices,
    in risk assessment 203–208, *204*;
    bioecological approach to information
    gathering *101*, 123–124; categories
    23–29; cultural factors 29; cultural
    intersection 59–60; cultural relativism *vs.*
    universalism 29–30; Cycle of Violence
    study 57–58; defining 22–39; differing
    views on 22; discipline *vs.* 22, 35–36;
    effects of 45–58; evaluating environment
    in 131; harmful cultural practices
    31–34; LGBTQ concerns in 150; long-
    term effects of 53, **54**; neglect 26, **28**;
    neuropsychological effects of 45–46,
    47; obstacles to assessment of 105–106,
    132–135; other cultural practices 36–37;
    and parental depression 70; parental
    intent 23; parent's history of 77–78; and
    personality disorders 55–56; physical
    abuse 24, **28**; protective factors for 85–88,
    86; psychological abuse 25, **28**; rates of
    2, 81; risk assessment 4; risk factors for
    70–85, *71*, **72–73**, 185–186, 187; sexual
    abuse 24, **28**; short-term effects of 46–53,
    48–49; socioeconomic cost of 58–59;
    type I *vs.* type II traumas 7, 44; unsafe
    living environments 27, **29**; US laws 23;
    see also decision making
Child Protective Services model 2
childrearing modes 173
children: age 81; Apollonian 174; assessing
    factors 107, 110, **111**; Athenian 176;
    attitudes toward 76, **108–109**, 124;

homophobia 153
honor killings 32
hostility 74
household violence 44
human psychosocial development, stages
  of 183, **185**
human trafficking, victims of 149
hypothalamic-pituitary-adrenal (HPA) axis
  45, **47**, 57

identity *vs.* role confusion stage **185**
immigrant parental stress 80
Immigrant Parental Stress Inventory
  (IPSI) 157
immigration/culture 12, 147
Implicit Association Test (IAT) 160
implicit biases 144, 160
impulsivity 74
incidents *vs.* symptoms 6–8, 120–121
individual child factors 147
Industrial Revolution 177
industry *vs.* inferiority stage **185**
infanticide mode 173
infibulation 31
initiative *vs.* guilt stage **185**
injuries: from neglect 49; from physical
  abuse 47; from sexual abuse 47, 49
insecure attachment 52, 59
Instrument for Identification of Parents
  at Risk for Child Abuse and Neglect
  (IPARAN) 114–115
intellectual disability 82
intensive parenting *see* child-centered
  parenting
intergenerational transmission, of
  maltreatment 77
internal locus of control 85
intersectionality theory 148
intimate partner violence (IPV) 27, 49–50,
  51, 57, 58, 74–75, 78
intrusion 24
intrusive mode 173, 174
intuitive thinking 195–197

Jenks, C. 174, 176
Jent, J. F. 10

Kahneman, D. 195–196
Kant, I. 201
Keating-Owen Child Labor Act
  (1916) 2
Klein, G. 196

labia majora 31
language barriers 156–157
LGBTQ people 142, 150; concerns 150,
  151; and ethnic culture 152–154; as
  sexual minority 151–152; status 82, 150,
  151; youth and maltreatment 150–154
limited insight, parents with 75
Locke, J. 175
Loftus, E. F. 130
long-term effects, of child
  maltreatment 53, **54**
love 183
'lowest threshold of parenting skills' 181
low intellectual functioning 75
low self-esteem, parents with 74

macrosystem 100, 124, 147
maltreatment: allegations 145; cultural
  factors in 29; discipline *vs.* 22; forms of
  23–29; LGBTQ youth and 150–151; *see
  also* child maltreatment
Masten, A. S. 89
maternal sociopathy 75
maturation and childhood 178
medical neglect 26
medical records 127
Memorandum of Good Practice
  (1992) 129
mental health: characteristics **111**;
  disorders **49**, 51, **108**; problems 73–74
mesosystem 100, 124, 147
metacolonialism 144
Mexican Parenting Questionnaire
  (MPQ) 157
microsystem 100, 115, 124, 147
mid-range families 179
Mill, J. S. 200
minimal parenting standards 172, 178, 181,
  206–207
Minnesota Multiphasic Personality
  Inventory-2 (MMPI-2) 111
minorities: double 152; ethnic/racial
  149–150, 152, 156; sexual 151–152
molestation, genital 24
moxibustion 37
multicultural assessment considerations
  154–160; disclosure of abuse 157–158;
  interacting with families 154–155;
  language barriers 156–157; symptom
  expression 159–160; views on parenting
  and abuse 158–159
multicultural ecological model 146–147

disorders **49**, 51; physical injuries
47, **48**, 49
sida-sida 153
Signs of Safety™ Model 199
sleeping arrangements 34–35
Smith, K. 176
social competence 87
social desirability bias 134
social isolation 84–85
socialization mode 173, 176
social learning theory 58
social proximal/wider systems
147
social sciences 142
social support 87–88, **112**
socioeconomic cost, of child
maltreatment 58–59
socioeconomic status (SES): disparities
in 10; environmental factors, assessing
83–84, **112**
socioemotional developmental needs,
children's 183
sociopathy 75
son preference 31–32
Sound Relationship House, theory of 180
sources of information 104–105, 122–124;
bioecological approach to information
gathering *101*, 123–124; child factors
107, 110, **128**; children and parents
assessment 122–123; collateral sources
104, 123; environmental factors 111,
131; parent factors 107, **125**; records
105, 122
Speight, A. P. 183
Sperry, L. 101, 121
spillover effects 78
Stages of Change model 186–187
standardized assessments 102, 121
stereotypes 14, 144, 146
stress 74, 76, 80
stressors, associated with culture 148–150
structure and stability, of family 77,
109
Structured Decision Making Model
(SDM) 199
Substance Abuse Subtle Screening
Inventory (SASSI) 111
substance use disorders 27, 58, 59, 71, 74,
75–76, **108**, 151, 187
Sudden Infant Death Syndrome
(SIDS) 34–35

suicidal ideation 150, 153
symptoms: dissociative 55; emotional/
behavioral 127, 128, 133, 159; evaluation
121, 127; expression 159–160; and
incidents 6–8, 120–121; and indicators
124; internalizing/externalizing 45, 49,
59, 87, 134; mental health 14, 55, 73,
74, 84, 89, 151, 153, 159; psychological
111, 120, 154, 159; PTSD 7, 56, 80;
resulting from child abuse and neglect
120; somatic 14, 53, 159; traumas 53, 56,
121, 159

tabula rasa 175
Taylor, J. 207
Tekin, E. 58
temperaments 82
Terr, L. C. 44
third gender 153, 154
Titterton, M. 207
transgender people 151, 153–154
transgenerational trauma 159
trauma: chronic/multiple 53;
developmental disorder 52–53, 56, 121;
symptoms of transgenerational 159;
type I 7, 44; type II 7, 44, 56; *see also*
posttraumatic stress disorder
(PTSD)
trust *vs.* mistrust stage **185**
type I traumas 7, 44
type II traumas 7, 44, 56

UN Convention on the Rights of the
Child 203
universalism 30
unsafe living environments, provision
of 27, **29**
Upsherin 36
US child maltreatment laws 23
utilitarianism, Mill's 200–201

verbal abuse 25
violence: challenges in assessing risk of
6; cycle of 57–58; domestic 27; family
5, 7, 78, 186; family rejection and
154; household 44; intergenerational
77; intimate partner 27, 49–50, 51,
57, 58, 74–75, 78; neglect and 44;
parent's history of 78, **109**; physical 58;
predicting 105
virginity testing 32–33

For Product Safety Concerns and Information please contact our EU
representative GPSR@taylorandfrancis.com
Taylor & Francis Verlag GmbH, Kaufingerstraße 24, 80331 München, Germany

www.ingramcontent.com/pod-product-compliance
Lightning Source LLC
Chambersburg PA
CBHW050351270326
41926CB00016B/3690

9 780367 464042